PR 2302 LYL

D1380697

QM Library

23 1302753 4

MAIN LIBRARY
QUEEN MARY, UNIVERSITY OF LONDON
Mile End Road, London E1 4NS

DATE DUE FOR RETURN.

NEW ACCESSIONS

CANCELLED

WITHDRAWN
FROM STOCK
QMUL LIBRARY

THE REVELS PLAYS

Former general editors
Clifford Leech
F. David Hoeniger
E. A. J. Honigmann
Eugene M. Waith

General editors
David Bevington, Richard Dutton, Alison Findlay,
J. R. Mulryne and Helen Ostovich

LOVE'S
METAMORPHOSIS

Manchester University Press

THE REVELS PLAYS

THE REVELS PLAYS

LOVE'S METAMORPHOSIS

JOHN LYLY

edited by Leah Scragg

MANCHESTER
UNIVERSITY PRESS

Manchester and New York

*distributed exclusively in the USA
by* Palgrave Macmillan

Introduction, critical apparatus, etc.
© Leah Scragg 2008

The right of Leah Scragg to be identified as the editor of this
work has been asserted by her in accordance with the Copyright,
Designs and Patents Act 1988.

Published by Manchester University Press
Oxford Road, Manchester M13 9NR, UK
and Room 400, 175 Fifth Avenue, New York, NY 10010, USA
www.manchesteruniversitypress.co.uk

Distributed exclusively in the USA by
Palgrave Macmillan, 175 Fifth Avenue, New York,
NY 10010, USA

Distributed exclusively in Canada by
UBC Press, University of British Columbia, 2029 West Mall,
Vancouver, BC, Canada V6T 1Z2

British Library Cataloguing-in-Publication Data
A catalogue record for this book is available from
the British Library

Library of Congress Cataloging-in-Publication Data applied for

ISBN   978 0 7190 7246 8 *hardback*

First published 2008

17 16 15 14 13 12 11 10 09 08   10 9 8 7 6 5 4 3 2 1

ONL LIBRARY
(MILE END)

Typeset in Plantin
by SNP Best-set Typesetter Ltd., Hong Kong
Printed in Great Britain
by Biddles Ltd, King's Lynn

Dedicated to the memory of
George K. Hunter
died 2008

Contents

General Editors' Preface

Clifford Leech conceived of the Revels Plays as a series in the mid-1950s, modelling the project on the New Arden Shakespeare. The aim, as he wrote in 1958, was 'to apply to Shakespeare's predecessors, contemporaries and successors the methods that are now used in Shakespeare's editing'. The plays chosen were to include well-known works from the early Tudor period to about 1700, as well as others less familiar but of literary and theatrical merit: 'the plays included', Leech wrote, 'should be such as to deserve and indeed demand performance'. We owe it to Clifford Leech that the idea became reality. He set the high standards of the series, ensuring that editors of individual volumes produced work of lasting merit, equally useful for teachers and students, theatre directors and actors. Clifford Leech remained General Editor until 1971, and was succeeded by F. David Hoeniger, who retired in 1985.

From 1985 the Revels Plays were under the direction of four General Editors: initially David Bevington, E. A. J. Honigmann, J. R. Mulryne and E. M. Waith. E. A. J. Honigmann retired in 2000 and was succeeded by Richard Dutton. E. M. Waith retired in 2003 and was succeeded by Alison Findlay and Helen Ostovich. Published originally by Methuen, the series is now published by Manchester University Press, embodying essentially the same format, scholarly character and high editorial standards of the series as first conceived. The series concentrates on plays from the period 1558–1642, and includes a small number of non-dramatic works of interest to students of drama. Some slight changes have been made: for example, in editions from 1978 onward, notes to the introduction are placed together at the end, not at the foot of the page. Collation and commentary notes continue, however, to appear on the relevant pages.

The text of each Revels play, in accordance with established practice in the series, is edited afresh from the original text of best authority (in a few instances, texts), but spelling and punctuation are modernized and speech headings are silently made consistent. Elisions in the original are also silently regularized, except where metre would be affected by the change; since 1968 the '-ed' form is used for non-syllabic terminations in past tenses and past participles ('-'d' earlier), and '-èd' for syllabic ('-ed' earlier). The editor emends, as distinct from modernizes, the original only in instances where error is patent, or at least very probable, and correction persuasive. Act divisions are given only if they appear in the original or if the structure of the play clearly points to them. Those act and scene divisions not in the original are provided in small type. Square brackets are also used for any other additions to or changes in the stage directions of the original.

Revels Plays do not provide a variorum collation, but only those variants which require the critical attention of serious textual students. All departures of substance from 'copy-text' are listed, including any relineation and those changes in punctuation which involve to any degree a decision between alternative interpretations; but not such accidentals as turned letters, nor necessary additions to stage directions whose editorial nature is already made clear by the use of brackets. Press corrections in the 'copy-text' are likewise collated. Of later emendations of the text, only those are given which as alternative readings still deserve attention.

One of the hallmarks of the Revels Plays is the thoroughness of their annotations. Besides explaining the meaning of difficult words and passages, the editor provides comments on customs or usage, text or stage-business – indeed, on anything judged pertinent and helpful. Each volume contains an Index to the Commentary, in which particular attention is drawn to meanings for words not listed in *OED*, and (starting in 1996) an indexing of proper names and topics in the Introduction and Commentary.

The introduction to a Revels play assesses the authority of the 'copy-text' on which it is based, and discusses the editorial methods employed in dealing with it; the editor also considers the play's date and (where relevant) sources, together with its place in the work of the author and in the theatre of its time. Stage history is offered, and in the case of a play by an author not previously represented in the series a brief biography is given.

It is our hope that plays edited in this fashion will promote further scholarly and theatrical investigation of one of the richest periods in theatrical history.

DAVID BEVINGTON
RICHARD DUTTON
ALISON FINDLAY
J. R. MULRYNE
HELEN OSTOVICH

Acknowledgements

I am indebted to numerous scholars and institutions for assistance in the production of this edition. The British Academy awarded me a grant which enabled me to collate the five copies of the 1601 quarto held by libraries in the United States, and I am grateful both to them and the staff of all eleven libraries in which the thirteen extant copies of the quarto are preserved (the British Library, the Bodleian Library, the Pepys Library (Magdalene College, Cambridge), St Paul's Cathedral Library, the Victoria and Albert Museum, Worcester College (Oxford), the Folger Shakespeare Library (Washington), the Houghton Library (Harvard), the Huntington Library (San Marino, California), the Lilly Library (University of Indiana, Bloomington), and the Harry Ransom Research Center (University of Texas at Austin) for their assistance in bringing this project to fruition. Among the numerous friends and colleagues who have supplied me with help and advice, I am particularly grateful to William Stoneman for providing me with information on G2 of the Houghton Library copy of the quarto, Martin Wiggins for transcribing extracts from Edward Pudsey's commonplace book on my behalf and supplying me with information on the Houghton Library copy of *Old Fortunatus*, Z. Philip Ambrose for permission to reproduce the image that appears on p. xii (Vergil Solis, *Erysichthon*: in *Mythological Slide Collection*, www.uvm.edu/-classics/ mainpagelinks/ambrose/html), Sue Hall-Smith for her endeavours to uncover any post-Renaissance productions of the play, Brian Schneider for his very helpful contributions to the commentary, and Robin Griffin for his unflagging readiness to assist with points of information on classical subjects, and to supervise the translation of the Latin material in the text.

Once again, however, it is to the previous editors of Lyly's work in the Revels series, George K. Hunter and David Bevington, to whom I am most deeply indebted. Constant recourse to their editions has supplied me with guidance on how best to proceed at every stage, together with innumerable points of information. One could not wish for a more learned, helpful, and supportive General Editor than David Bevington, who has overseen the production of this volume.

Abbreviations

ABBREVIATIONS USED IN THE NOTES

bk	book
ed.	edited by
eds	editors
Gk	Greek
l./ll.	line/lines
n./nn.	note/notes
p./pp.	page/pages
Q	quarto (specifically the 1601 quarto of *Love's Metamorphosis*)
r	recto
rev.	revised
SD/SDs	stage direction/stage directions
SP	speech prefix
subst.	substantively
v	verso
vol./vols	volume/volumes

ANCIENT TEXTS

Wherever possible, Graeco-Roman texts are cited by the standard reference to book, chapter, and paragraph for prose texts, or to book (where applicable), poem, and line number for verse. All references to Ovid's *Metamorphoses* (*Met.*) are to the translation by Arthur Golding (1567), in the edition by W. H. D. Rouse, published as *Shakespeare's Ovid: being Arthur Golding's translation of the 'Metamorphoses'* (1904, reissued 1961), and are followed by the corresponding line numbers in the Loeb Classical Library (LCL) edition. LCL offers a convenient means of access to the work of many classical authors, and all other citations are to the most recent editions in the series, unless otherwise stated.

Juvenal, *Satires*	In *Juvenal and Persius*.
Ovid, *Am.*	*Amores*. In *Heroides: Amores*.
Ovid, *Ars am.*	*Ars amatoria*. In *The Art of Love and other Poems*.
Ovid, *Fa.*	*Fasti*.
Ovid, *Her.*	*Heroides*. In *Heroides: Amores*.
Ovid, *Rem. am.*	*Remedia amoris*. In *The Art of Love and other Poems*.
Pliny, *Hist. nat.*	*Historia naturalis*.
Virgil, *Eclogues*	In *Eclogues: Georgics: Aeneid I–VI*.

OTHER ABBREVIATIONS

The place of publication is London unless otherwise indicated. All quotations from the works of Shakespeare are from *The Arden Shakespeare Complete Works*, gen. eds Richard Proudfoot, Ann Thompson, and David Scott Kastan (1998, rev. 2001). Abbreviations of the works of Shakespeare are those adopted by the Revels Plays. References to plays other than those by Shakespeare are to the Revels editions.

Anatomy Euphues: The Anatomy of Wit. See Lyly.
Andreadis   A. Harriette Andreadis, ed., *Mother Bombie*, Elizabethan and Renaissance Studies (Salzburg, 1975).
Astington   John H. Astington, *English Court Theatre 1558–1642* (Cambridge, 1999).
Barish   Jonas Barish, 'The Prose Style of John Lyly', *ELH* 23 (1956), 14–35.
Bevington, ed., *Endymion*   See Lyly.
Bond   R. Warwick Bond, ed., *The Complete Works of John Lyly*, 3 vols (Oxford, 1902).
Croll and Clemons   Morris William Croll and Harry Clemons, eds, *Euphues: The Anatomy of Wit / Euphues and His England* (1916, reissued New York, 1964).
Daniel   Carter A. Daniel, ed., *The Plays of John Lyly* (Lewisburg, PA, 1988).
Dent   R. W. Dent, *Proverbial Language in English Drama Exclusive of Shakespeare, 1495–1616* (Berkeley and Los Angeles, 1984).
Dooley   Mark Dooley, 'The Healthy Body: Desire and Sustenance in John Lyly's *Love's Metamorphosis*', *Early Modern Literary Studies* 6.2 (2000).
Edge   Donald James Edge, *Critical Editions of John Lyly's 'Endymion' and 'Love's Metamorphosis'*, unpublished PhD dissertation (Rochester, New York, 1973).
England Euphues and His England. See Lyly.
Fairholt   F. W. Fairholt, ed., *The Dramatic Works of John Lilly*, 2 vols (1858).
Feuillerat   Albert Feuillerat, *Documents Relating to the Office of the Revels in the Time of Queen Elizabeth*, in *Materialien zur Kunde des alteren Englischen Dramas*, xxi (Louvain, 1908).
Greg   W. W. Greg, *A Bibliography of the English Printed Drama to the Restoration*, 4 vols (1939–59).
Hollis   A. S. Hollis, ed., *Ovid: 'Metamorphoses' Book VIII* (Oxford, 1970).
Houppert   Joseph W. Houppert, *John Lyly*, Twayne's English Authors Series (Boston, 1975).
Hunter   G. K. Hunter, *John Lyly: The Humanist as Courtier* (1962).
Hunter and Bevington, eds, *Campaspe: Sappho and Phao*   See Lyly.
Hunter and Bevington, eds, *Galatea: Midas*   See Lyly.
Lancashire   Anne Lancashire, 'John Lyly and Pastoral Entertainment', in G. R. Hibbard, ed., *The Elizabethan Theatre VIII* (Port Meany, 1982), pp. 22–50.

Lyly   References are to the Revels Plays (Manchester) for *Campaspe* and
    Sappho and Phao (ed. George K. Hunter and David Bevington, 1991),
    Endymion (ed. David Bevington, 1996), *Galatea* and *Midas* (ed. George
    K. Hunter and David Bevington, 2000), and *The Woman in the Moon*
    (ed. Leah Scragg, 2006). References to *Euphues: The Anatomy of Wit*
    and *Euphues and His England* are to the modern-spelling edition in the
    Revels Plays Companion Library Series (ed. Leah Scragg, Manchester,
    2003). All references to *Love's Metamorphosis* are to the present edition
    unless otherwise stated. References to *Mother Bombie* are to Bond,
    except where Andreadis is specifically cited.
McKerrow   R. B. McKerrow and F. S. Ferguson, *Title-page Borders Used
    in England and Scotland 1485–1640* (1932).
OED   *The Oxford English Dictionary*.
Onions   C. T. Onions, *A Shakespeare Glossary*, enlarged and rev. Robert D.
    Eagleson (Oxford, 1986).
Parnell   Paul E. Parnell, 'Moral Allegory in Lyly's *Loves* [*sic*] *Metamorpho-
    sis*', *Studies in Philology* LII (1955), 1–16.
Pincombe   Michael Pincombe, *The Plays of John Lyly: Eros and Eiza*, Revels
    Plays Companion Library Series (Manchester, 1996).
Saccio   Peter Saccio, *The Court Comedies of John Lyly: A Study in Allegorical
    Dramaturgy* (Princeton, NJ, 1969).
Scragg   Leah Scragg, *The Metamorphosis of 'Gallathea': A Study in Creative
    Adaptation* (Washington, DC, 1982).
STC   A. W. Pollard and G. R. Redgrave, *A Short-Title Catalogue of Books
    Printed in England, Scotland, and Ireland . . . 1475–1640*, rev., W. A.
    Jackson, F. S. Ferguson, and K. F. Pantzer, 3 vols (1976–91).
Tilley   Morris Palmer Tilley, *A Dictionary of the Proverbs in England in the
    Sixteenth and Seventeenth Centuries* (Ann Arbor, 1950).

Vergil Solis, *Erysichthon* (1563)

Introduction

Love's Metamorphosis is first mentioned in a Stationers' Register entry for 1600:

> 25. Nouembris
>
> **wᵐ wood** Entred for his Copie vnder the handes of Mʳ Pasfeild and the wardens A booke Called Loves metamorphesis wrytten by mʳ Iohn Lylly and playd by the Children of Paules   vjᵈ.[1]

The play was published in the course of the next year, with the following title-page:

> LOVES META-MORPHOSIS. [within lace border] / *A* / VVittie and Courtly / Pastorall, / VVRITTEN BY / *Mr. Iohn Lyllie.* / First playd by the Children of Paules, and now / by the Children of the Chappell. / [device, McKerrow 331] / LONDON / Printed for William Wood, dwelling at the West end of / Paules, at the signe of Time. 1601.

No printer is mentioned on the title-page, but the device on B1r (McKerrow 295𝔅) links the play with *George a Greene* (1599), and the shop of Simon Stafford.[2]

The text collates [A]2 B–F4 G2 (C–F fully signed) and has twenty-four unnumbered leaves, the title-page being on A2r (A1 and A2v blank). Act 1 begins on B1r, below the device identified as Stafford's, and the title of the play in large type, but with no act or scene heading. The play concludes with '*FINIS*' on G1r, the final page bearing a device (McKerrow 312), in place of a colophon, depicting the figure of Time, which alludes, like the smaller version of the same woodcut on the title-page (McKerrow 331), to the sign of the publisher's shop.[3] The text is cleanly printed, with very few typographical errors, but for the omission of one speech prefix (on E1r: 4.1.135),[4] one instance of confusion between names (Niobe and Nisa, on F3v: 5.4.110), the possible loss of a negative (on E2v: 4.2.69), six probable misreadings (on B2v, E3v, E4v, F4v (2), and G1r: 1.2.44, 5.1.11, 5.1.71, 5.4.166, 5.4.170, and 5.4.183), and three mistakes in the numbering of scenes (ACTVS QVARTVS. SCENA PRIMA for ACTVS QVARTVS. SCENA SECVNDA on E1v,

I

ACTVS QVINTVS. SCENA PRIMA for ACTVS QVINTVS. SCENA SECVNDA on E4v, and ACTVS QVINTVS. SCENA QVARTA for ACTVS QVINTUS. SCENA TERTIA on F1v). Collation of the thirteen extant copies[5] reveals no press variants.

Like the majority of Lylian comedies published during the dramatist's lifetime, the layout of the text is conspicuously orderly and consistent, suggesting that the play either was prepared by the writer himself for publication[6] or was 'very close to what Lyly had written'.[7] The names of the characters are grouped together at the head of each scene on the classical model, rather than being specified as entrances occur, and the order in which the names are printed does not always conform to that in which the characters speak (e.g. in 1.2, and the concluding scene). As in all Lyly's plays with the exception of *The Woman in the Moon*,[8] stage directions are notably sparse.[9] Singing and dancing are signalled in large type on B2v ('*Cantant & Saltant*': 1.2.67.1), a further song is indicated, again in large type, on C4v ('*Cantant*': 3.1.147.1), and the behaviour of the Siren is precisely denoted ('*Sing with a Glasse in her hand and a Combe*': E2r: 4.2.51.1), but none of the play's major spectacles (e.g. the felling of the arborified Fidelia on B4r / 1.2.156.1, or the transformatory shower that restores the nymphs to their own shapes on F2v / 5.4.39–43.1) is accorded a direction.[10] Mid-scene entrances are unspecified, and mid-scene exits are frequently omitted (e.g. on C3v / 3.1.80 and 84, and C4v / 3.1.147.1), while there is no textual indication when characters are required to speak *sotto voce* or aside (e.g. on E2v: 4.2.61). The songs that punctuate the action are not included in the text, an omission common to all the Lylian quartos with the exception of *The Woman in the Moon*, while the many props required in the course of the action (e.g. garlands and 'scutcheons' in 1.1, an axe in 1.2, doves in 2.1 etc.) are not specified in the directions. Taken together, the evidence suggests that the copy from which the play was printed derived from the playwright rather than the playhouse (cf. the cluster of Lylian comedies issued by William Broome and his widow subsequent to the closure of Paul's Boys), though Lyly's close involvement in the production of his own plays may well have obviated the need to mark up his work for production, minimizing the distinction between the two kinds of text.[11]

Though *Love's Metamorphosis* shares the characteristics of the majority of Lylian quartos, however, it differs markedly from them in terms of its length. Whereas *Sappho and Phao* has 1,681 type lines (excluding catch words), *Galatea* 1,729, and *Mother Bombie* 2,153,

Love's Metamorphosis has only 1,264,[12] and the brevity of the drama distinguishes it from all of the other seven plays that with it make up the Lylian corpus. The shortness of the piece is ascribable to the lack of a sub-plot concerned with the activities of a group of witty apprentices or young servants, a device characteristic of Lyly's work,[13] inviting the supposition that the quarto represents an abbreviated version of the text; and the possibility that the play has been subject to some process of abridgement (discussed more fully below) is strengthened by the increasing spaciousness with which the quarto is set out. Whereas quires B, C, and D are comparatively crowded, with circa 36 type lines (excluding catch words) per page, from E1r the number of lines decreases, while headings are more widely spaced. E1r, for example, concludes mid-page, after only twenty-one lines, while E4v has only twenty-seven lines, and F1r twenty-eight. F1v begins, unusually, with a heavy black line below the title, after a wide space, and similar wide spaces separate the act and scene headings and the names of the dramatis personae from the ensuing speech, leaving only nineteen lines of text; while F2r is equally widely spaced, with only twenty lines of text (including the act and scene headings and a two-line list of the characters' names). The uneven distribution of the material, taken together with the misnumbering of scenes in Acts 4 and 5, may suggest some disruption in the printer's copy, but the argument is far from conclusive, and the more generous spacing may merely arise from a growing realization on the part of the printer of the need to expand his material into a new quire.

While the misnumbering of scenes and more ample spacing may point to adaptation, they may equally be adduced as evidence that more than one compositor was at work. In the only detailed bibliographical analysis of the quarto,[14] Donald Edge argues that the 'repeated scene headings on the outer and inner formes of quires D and E' together with 'the confused scene heading on the inner forme of quire F (F1v)' indicate that the quarto was the work of at least two compositors, 'setting by formes from cast-off copy', and that this position is supported by the marked variation of practice in the layout of the text. He compares the large type and wide spacing of the expansive stage direction indicating that the Siren sings on E2r (inner forme), '*Sing with a Glasse in her hand and a Combe*', with the terse '*Sing againe Syren*' in much smaller type on the highly congested E2v (outer forme), which, 'although it interrupts a speech of Petulius . . . is not printed on a separate line'. Once again, however, the evidence is susceptible of other explanations. Similar errors in scene numbering in *Sappho and Phao* and *Mother Bombie*[15] point to some difficulty in interpreting the dramatist's method of numeration, while, as Edge himself notes: 'much of the white space . . . may originate in an attempt to expand a slight text into marketable length'.

Love's Metamorphosis was not reprinted during the dramatist's lifetime, and the play was not among the group of comedies registered to Edward Blount in 1628 and published by him, in the first collected edition of Lyly's plays (*Six Court Comedies*), in 1632. A number of passages from the play are noted, however, in a contemporary commonplace book (Bodleian manuscript Eng. Poet d. 3), to be discussed more fully in relation to the play's date, but they do not differ significantly from the text published by Wood. It is consequently upon the 1601 quarto that the present edition is based (see 'This Edition' below).[16]

AUTHORSHIP AND DATE

Love's Metamorphosis is one of only two plays by Lyly to carry his name on the title page,[17] and his authorship is supported by the entry in the Stationers' Register quoted on p. 1 above, and by the attribution of a number of passages from the play to him, in conjunction with a further quotation from his first play, *Campaspe*, in the commonplace book of Edward Pudsey (1573–1613),[18] in which extracts are noted from a large number of Elizabethan and Jacobean plays.[19] Though the piece was not included in Blount's 1632 edition of the dramatist's comedies, and the work is considerably shorter than the majority of Lyly's plays (see pp. 2–3 above), his authorship has been universally accepted, and is confirmed by a wealth of internal evidence. The action turns, like that of *Sappho and Phao*, *Galatea*, and *Endymion*, upon the tension between love and chastity, and evolves, in common with the Lylian canon as a whole, through a pattern of oppositions (see pp. 17ff. below). The dialogue, as in all Lyly's plays, is remote from natural speech, exhibiting the antithetical balance, word-play, and heavy reliance upon proverbial lore and classical allusion characteristic of euphuistic prose. The work evokes an unstable universe in which everything is subject to change, with the malleability of mind and matter insistently enforced through the dramatic language, explicitly asserted (cf. *Galatea*, 1.1.22ff. and *Love's Metamorphosis*, 1.2.5–7), and visually realized through the

stage spectacles that the dramatist engineers (cf. the on-stage transformation of the arborified Bagoa in *Endymion,* and the nymphs'
recovery, in *Love's Metamorphosis,* of their human forms). The cast
is tailored, as always in Lyly's work,[20] to the capabilities of the
juvenile troupe for which the piece was designed (see p. 39 below),
with a preponderance of youthful roles,[21] and opportunities for
dancing (e.g. at 1.2.67.1) and song (e.g. at 3.1.147.1 and 4.2.51.1).
Echoes of other items in the Lylian corpus are detectable, moreover,
throughout. Images that occur in *Euphues: The Anatomy of Wit* and
Euphues and His England are regularly deployed (e.g. at 1.2.46–7,
1.2.53–4, 4.1.109–11, and 4.2.86–7: *Anatomy,* pp. 219, 61, 30 /
England, p. 157); exchanges from *Campaspe* (1.1.50–6 and 2.2.163–
4) are recalled in the encounter between Protea and the Merchant
(3.2.70–9); while the words of the aged Sybilla to Phao in *Sappho
and Phao* (2.4.61ff.) are echoed at 4.1.125–31 and 146–7. In addition,
a series of direct allusions to *Galatea* invites the audience to view
the play in terms of a continuum of work. The subjection of Diana's
nymphs to love through the agency of Cupid, for example, central
to the action of *Galatea,* is adduced by Ceres, at 2.1.87–92, as evidence of the god's power over the most chaste, and recalled by
Cupid himself at 5.1.21, while the two plays are linked by an implied
debate over whether Cupid is a great or a little god.[22] A host of
further correspondences signals the close relationship between the
two works, suggesting that one is directly structured upon the other,
and may be regarded, in some sense, as a companion piece.[23] The
action is set in both cases in a pastoral location, adjacent to a sea-
coast, and turns upon the mollification of an offended deity (Neptune
/ Ceres) whose place of worship has been desecrated, and the punishment of a group of nymphs, dedicated to chastity, who have
slighted Cupid's power. The situation is resolved through the transformatory power of love, literalized through a metamorphosis
effected by Venus, while the instability of the world in which the
events of the two dramas take place is linked to the figure of Neptune,
who is capable of effecting change at will. A principal site of the
action of both works is a tree dedicated to one of the major deities
of the world of the play (Neptune / Ceres), which is at once a place
of reverence and the arena for the death of an innocent virgin (Hebe
/ Fidelia),[24] who laments her untimely fate at length (cf. *Galatea,*
5.2.8–60 and *Love's Metamorphosis,* 1.2.107–54). Given that *Galatea*
itself looks back to *Sappho and Phao,* in which Venus' son plays
a central role,[25] the links between the former play and *Love's*

Metamorphosis may be seen as locating the latter in a sequence of closely related works, concerned with the status of Cupid and exploring the nature of his power.

While serving to confirm Lyly's authorship of the work, the affinity between *Love's Metamorphosis* and the second and third of Lyly's court comedies appears to offer a straightforward indication of the period of the dramatist's career during which the play was composed. Though there is no record of a performance of *Galatea* before 1588, the evidence suggests that it was written, like *Sappho and Phao*, prior to the closure of the first Blackfriars theatre, and the fact that it was entered in the Stationers' Register in 1585[26] supports other indications that it belongs to the first phase of Lyly's theatrical career. If *Love's Metamorphosis* was indeed designed as the third of a series of closely related plays, it clearly may be assigned to the same period, and may well have been written (though not necessarily performed) before the demise of the first Blackfriars in 1584.

A number of factors, however, complicate this chronology, leading to wide discrepancies in the dates that commentators have assigned to the work.[27] Although *Galatea* was undoubtedly in existence by 1585, there is no record, as noted above, that it was performed before 1588, and the fact that it was not published, like Lyly's two previous plays, *Campaspe* and *Sappho and Phao*, immediately following the closure of the Blackfriars may suggest that the piece had yet to be staged when the company broke up, and thus that there would have been no call for a companion piece. The writing of *Love's Metamorphosis* may consequently follow not the composition of the earlier play but its first performance at court, pushing the date of the later work forward into the middle period of the dramatist's career. Echoes of the play in *Midas*, a political allegory celebrating the defeat of the Spanish Armada, confirm that *Love's Metamorphosis* was in the dramatist's mind at this time, adding weight to the contention that the play was written circa 1588.[28]

Though running counter to the concept of *Sappho and Phao*, *Galatea*, and *Love's Metamorphosis* as a creative unit, the argument that the play was written towards the end rather than the beginning of the decade appears to be supported by a number of similarities between the comedy and a cluster of works written towards the close of the 1580s. There are parallels, for example, between the fate of Fradubio and Fraelissa in book i, canto 2 of *The Fairie Queene* (1589) and that of Fidelia in 1.2 of Lyly's play, while Bond suggests that Lyly's description of Famine 'might be modelled on Spenser's similar pictures of Idleness, Gluttony, Wrath etc.'.[29] More extensive parallels have been traced, moreover, between *Love's Metamorphosis* and Greene's *Alcida*, licensed in 1588, leading a number of scholars to the conclusion that Greene's work offers irrefutable evidence of the terminus a quo of Lyly's play.[30] The relationship between the drama and the two non-dramatic works does not provide an incontrovertible answer, however, to the many problems surrounding the date of the work. The principal source of *Love's Metamorphosis* is universally agreed to be book viii of Ovid's *Metamorphoses* (discussed in more detail under 'Sources' below), and the similarities between Lyly's description of Famine and the corresponding passage of Ovid's text are too extensive to admit the possibility of Lyly's indebtedness to another source (see 2.1.12–14 and 22–31nn. below).[31] Similarly, the arborification of a nubile young woman has numerous parallels in Ovid's work, while the situation of Fidelia, transformed at her own request to escape a rape, does not correspond with that of Fraelissa, whose situation is the product of malice. Lyly's dependence on Greene's work is equally open to doubt. Though there are a number of points of similarity between the two, from the metamorphosis of a group of young women to some verbal resemblances in a specific area of the two texts (see 3.1.119–38n.), Edge has convincingly demonstrated that the case for indebtedness may be argued either way,[32] and that it is equally likely that Greene borrowed from Lyly as that Lyly borrowed from Greene[33] – an argument that gains weight from the obvious parallels between *Alcida* and other items in the Lylian canon.[34] The resemblances between the two texts may thus be taken as an indication that, rather than following *Alcida*, *Love's Metamorphosis* was in existence before the composition of the non-dramatic work, and either that Greene had seen the play in performance or that it circulated in some form prior to the first extant quarto of 1601.

The late publication of *Love's Metamorphosis* adds a further layer of complication to the problems surrounding the date of the play. Following the demise of Paul's Boys circa 1590, the texts of the majority of Lyly's court comedies passed into the hands of William and Joan Broome, who published five of the eight plays now attributed to him between 1591 and 1592.[35] Though both *Sappho and Phao* and *Galatea* are among this group of works, *Love's Metamorphosis* was neither among those listed in the relevant entry in the Stationers' Register, nor those published by either Broome himself or his widow in the course of 1591–92. The omission invites the supposition that, contrary to the argument advanced above, the play was not composed until the latter half of the 1590s, when playing resumed at Paul's, or that it had become separated, at some point in its history, from the remainder of the Lylian corpus. The latter argument is supported by the similar histories of *Mother Bombie* and *The Woman in the Moon*, both of which may antedate the closure of Paul's Boys, but which do not appear until 1594 and 1597 respectively. The information supplied on the title-page of the work, when it was finally published by William Wood in 1601, 'First playd by the Children of Paules, and now by the Children of the Chappell', also adds weight to this proposition, in that it indicates that the play changed hands in the course of its history, passing from one company of boys to another. On closer inspection, however, the wording poses a further set of problems that have yet to be satisfactorily resolved. The work is advertised as '*A* Wittie and Courtly Pastorall, WRITTEN BY *Mr. Iohn Lyllie*', an announcement which firmly locates the play within the Lylian corpus, but adds, simultaneously, new dimensions of uncertainty to the history of the text. Whereas the title-pages of the group of comedies published by William and Joan Broome in 1591–92 directly assert that all five items were played before the Queen, the phrasing of the preliminary matter of *Love's Metamorphosis* is more evasive, stressing the 'courtly' nature of the drama, rather than that it had been performed in the Queen's presence. The statement may suggest that, though written in the *mode* of Lyly's court comedies ('*A* Wittie and Courtly Pastorall'), it was not staged, in fact, before the Queen, though a royal performance may well have been envisaged at the time of composition.[36] The closure of the first Blackfriars theatre and the dissolution of Paul's Boys would both explain the possible failure of the play to reach its intended audience, though it is difficult to understand why, had the play been written for the former venue, it was not performed at court, like *Galatea*, at a later date.[37]

The claim that the play was 'First playd by the Children of Paules, and now by the Children of the Chappell' also opens up a number of channels of speculation. The title-pages of all Lyly's plays, with the exception of *The Woman in the Moon*, carry some form of announcement that the work was performed by Paul's Boys, either alone (e.g. *Endymion* and *Midas*) or in conjunction with another troupe (e.g. *Campaspe* and *Sappho and Phao*). The mention of Paul's Boys thus serves to associate the play with other items in the Lylian canon, but fails to shed light on the difficult question of when the play was composed. Given that the playhouse in Paul's ceased to function circa 1590, only to be revived towards the end of the decade, the statement that the piece was performed by the troupe may refer to either a recent or distant event. At the same time, the phrasing 'First playd by the Children of Paules, and *now* by the Children of the Chappell' (my italics) points to two distinct phases in the history of the work, indicating that the quarto follows a recent performance by the second of the two troupes. Given that Paul's did not reopen until the latter end of the decade, it seems highly unlikely, as Edge notes (p. 57), that, had they produced the play subsequent to their revival, it would then have been acquired and performed by a different company in the brief period before the play was licensed for publication. It would therefore seem probable that the play was initially performed by Paul's Boys prior to their closure, and subsequently revived, towards the close of the 1590s, by the Children of the Chapel, who sold it for publication once its potential for drawing audiences was exhausted. No mention is made, however, of the Chapel Children in the relevant entry in Stationers' Register (see p. 1 above), which simply states that the piece was 'playd by the Children of Paules', and it is hard to supply an explanation for a play being attributed in the Register to one company after it had been sold for publication by another.

There is no record of any other play by Lyly having changed hands prior to publication, and the company's apparent readiness to part with the work, coupled with the shortness of the text, have led to the assumption by some commentators that it excited the hostile notice of the authorities, and was consequently subject to censorship. Bond suggests, for example, that 'it contained some matter, perhaps of Anti-Martinist tendency, which was sufficient to prevent the play obtaining its licence for printing along with *Endimion*, *Gallathea*, and *Midas* in 1591', and that the play, 'as revived, whether by the Paul's or Chapel Children, was an alteration from that originally produced'.[38] The play that has come down to us is thus very different, in his view, from that which was originally composed, and is rich in topical references to events at the close of the 1590s.[39] Though the argument that the work was revised may help to explain some of the confusion in the scene headings of the quarto, there is no firm evidence that the play was subject to censorship, or obvious scope within it for anti-Martinist material,[40] while the supposed topical references (discussed more fully on pp. 29–31 below) are tenuous in the extreme. Others have argued, moreover, that, rather than being a truncated text, *Love's Metamorphosis* is an experimental work,[41] and may be compared with similar short pieces of uncertain date, possibly written for Paul's Boys immediately prior to their closure, and revised for the same company at a later date.[42]

On the basis of the foregoing, it can be stated with some certainty that *Love's Metamorphosis* was written shortly after *Galatea*, and prior to the composition of *Midas*. It was performed by Paul's Boys, probably before their dissolution circa 1590, and revived by the Children of the Chapel towards the close of the decade. Though the rest of its history is clouded in uncertainty, there are, in addition, some indications of its turn-of-the-century reception. A number of names, the use of emphatic patterning (particularly in formalized expressions of love), and some verbal echoes link the play with *As You Like It*,[43] suggesting that its revival attracted the notice of the later dramatist, while extracts from the work in Pudsey's commonplace book (see p. 4 above) confirm its interest for contemporary spectators. A derisive remark by Jonson in the Induction to *Cynthia's Revels*, also performed by the Chapel Children in 1600 and published like *Love's Metamorphosis* in 1601, has been widely construed, moreover, as a reflection on Lyly's play. Jonson comments on the fact that 'the *umbrae*, or ghosts of some three or foure playes, departed a dozen yeeres since, haue bin seene walking on your stage heere' and that if indeed the playhouse 'bee haunted with such *hobgoblins*, 'twill fright away all your spectators' (194–8).[44] The jibe has been taken as indicative that Lyly's work was no longer in fashion,[45] but it might equally be read as the disgruntled comment of a young writer, still in process of establishing himself, at finding tried and trusted material preferred before new work. *Plus ça change . . .*

SOURCES

The immediate source of the story that supplies the nexus of the three interrelated strands of the plot of *Love's Metamorphosis* is Ovid's *Metamorphoses*, bk viii, which relates the felling of a grove sacred to Ceres by Erisichthon, causing the death of an arborified nymph; the insatiable hunger visited upon the malefactor as a punishment for his sacrilegious act; his sale of his daughter in order to feed himself when his means are exhausted; and the latter's eluding of her purchasers through her capacity to change shape (lines 923–1088 / LCL, 738–878). The origins of the tale are much older, however, than the Ovidian text upon which Lyly draws.[46] Erisich-thon's insatiable hunger and sale of his protean daughter are first recorded by Hesiod in *The Catalogues of Women*, and there are numerous early witnesses to the same tradition. Ovid himself drew on Callimachus' *Hymn to Demeter*, but he may also have been famil-iar with a variety of other versions of the story, which appears to have survived in the oral tradition, on the island of Cos, until modern times.[47] The close proximity between Lyly's play and the Ovidian text (e.g. in the description of Famine at 2.1.22–31 and *Met.*, viii, 994–1004 / LCL, 801–8) leaves no room for doubt, however, that the latter was Lyly's principal source, though he departs from the poem in a number of respects. Whereas Ovid describes the destruction of a whole grove of trees by Erisichthon's servants, one of whom is killed by his master for resisting his com-mands, in Lyly's play the action is focused upon a single tree, which is woven into another strand of the plot, and which itself carries echoes of Ovid in that it turns on the metamorphosis of a trio of nymphs.[48] Erisichthon's daughter, Mestra in the classical tradition but unnamed in the poem, is assigned a name, Protea, indicative of her capacity to change form, while the patronage bestowed upon her by Neptune arises not from his rape of her but from her seduc-tion. Rather than dying by autophagy as in Ovid, Erisichthon is eventually pardoned by Ceres, allowing for a harmonious resolution through love and forgiveness in place of the dire warning against sacrilegious conduct offered by the poem.

The most important distinction between the treatment of the inherited story by the two writers, however, lies in its positioning within the structure of the work. Whereas in Ovid the tale of Erisi-chthon is told as a further example of the ability to change shape, re-enforcing the universal fluidity at the heart of the poem, in the Lylian drama the story is woven into a network of interests turning upon a definition of love, and exhibiting its transformatory nature. Thus in Act 1, the tree which Erisichthon is later to fell is the site of a ritual in honour of Ceres, in the course of which three nymphs (Nisa, Celia, and Niobe) repudiate the love of three foresters (Ramis, Montanus, and Silvestris), prompting the maidens' transformation by Cupid, and Ceres' ensuing remission of Erisichthon's punish-ment in return for the restoration of her nymphs; while in Act 4, Erisichthon's daughter, Protea, not only saves her father's life by her capacity to change shape but rescues her lover, Petulius, by the same means, from the wiles of a Siren. At the same time, material

drawn from the dramatist's previous compositions is woven into the
fabric of the work. The Lucilla of *The Anatomy of Wit* combines the
characteristics of the nymphs of the play, in that she is beautiful,
witty, and fickle, while the predicament of the three foresters in
relation to their beautiful but cold, mocking, and inconstant mistresses carries echoes of the 'question' posed by Iffida to Fidus in
Euphues and His England as to whether he would prefer a fair fool,
a witty wanton, or a saintly cripple for his wife (pp. 205–9).[49] More
significantly, the Ovidian story is located, as noted above, in a continuum of Lylian plays turning upon the tension between love and
chastity, and the nature and status of Cupid. In *Sappho and Phao*,
the first of the series, the boy god, Cupid, defects from the service
of his domineering mother, Venus, and devotes himself to Sappho
(i.e. Elizabeth), figuring the monarch's control over her amatory
instincts; while in *Galatea*, upon which *Love's Metamorphosis* is more
closely structured (see pp. 5–6 above), one of the nymphs of Diana
derides Cupid as a 'little god' (1.2.32), prompting his exhibition of
his power over the followers of the virgin huntress, all of whom fall
victim to love, but who, in turn, revenge themselves on him following his capture by extinguishing his brands, breaking his bow, and
clipping his wings – allowing for a resolution in which Venus and
Diana play an equal part. The process of reversal at work in the
three plays in the relative status of love and chastity is completed in
Love's Metamorphosis. It is now Cupid, no longer a child subservient
to his mother but a potent deity in his own right, who is the most
powerful of the play's authority figures, and Ceres, embodiment of
chastity, who defers to him and counsels her followers to heed his
advice. The Ovidian tale thus no longer functions as a further
instance of a universal condition but forms part of an evolving
debate turning on a subject which, for all the classical origins of the
play, is of direct relevance to the Elizabethan court (see pp. 28–31
below).

The promotion of the play as a 'Courtly Pastorall' on the title-
page of the 1601 quarto locates the work in a yet wider network of
influences and traditions.[50] The rural setting, the pastoral and mythological figures, highly patterned dialogue, and opportunities for
song and dance all situate the comedy within the parameters of a
type of entertainment that enjoyed a considerable vogue among the
intelligentsia in the latter half of the sixteenth century, and was the
staple of the royal progress. Set either in Arcadia itself or in a comparable golden age world, governed by classical deities, peopled by

shepherds, foresters, or nymphs, engaged with varieties of amatory experience, and highly non-naturalistic in style, the pastoral informed during this period a wide range of literary modes,[51] and offered a ready vehicle in its idealized setting and susceptibility to allegorical treatment for the celebration of the sovereign, contributing to the cult of the virgin queen. During Elizabeth's visit to Kenilworth, for example, in 1575, the parkland became the arena for a host of entertainments, in the course of which she encountered a variety of mythological figures, including Sylvanus (cf. Lyly's Silvestris), who narrated a love story, and Nature, who lamented her departure; while at Woodstock in the same year she was entertained with a tale by a hermit, and music and song proceeding from an oak tree (cf. Fidelia's speech delivered from Ceres' tree in *Love's Metamorphosis*, 1.2). In Wanstead garden in 1578, she was called upon to judge a contest between a shepherd and a forester, while at Cowdray in 1591 she was conducted to a tree hung with escutcheons (cf. *Love's Metamorphosis*, 1.1), and addressed by 'a wilde man cladde in Iuie'[52] who expounded the allegorical significance of the event.

A high proportion of Lyly's plays are indebted in some measure to the pastoral tradition, contributing, in turn, to its popularity at court.[53] *Sappho and Phao*, for example, includes a number of classical deities and a simple ferryman among the dramatis personae, and opens with one of the conventional debate topoi of the genre, a comparison between court and country; while *Galatea* is set throughout in a pastoral location inhabited by nymphs and shepherds, and overseen by the classical gods, and is both concerned with amatory matters and highly patterned in its design. Of all Lyly's court comedies, however, it is *Love's Metamorphosis* which adheres most closely to the conventions of the genre. Unlike *Sappho and Phao* in which a number of scenes are set in the vicinity of the court (including the bedroom of the Queen), the action takes place exclusively in 'pastoral' locations (a grove, a sea-shore, the forecourt of a temple), while its divorce from everyday life is heightened by the use of overt patterning, both within and between speeches, and in the structure of the action as a whole (see pp. 17ff. below). Similarly, whereas in *Galatea* three recognizably Elizabethan apprentices weave their way through the work in search of a master, no figures extraneous to the delocalized pastoral arena, remote from any specific temporal reality, intrude into the world of the play, or distract from its amatory concerns. Nevertheless, though the strict adherence to the conventions of the genre invites the audience to locate the work within the context of the pastoral tradition, the dramatist departs from his inherited mode in a number of respects. None of Lyly's lovers, for example, conforms to an ideal of unqualified, virginal commitment (cf. Protea's seduction by Neptune, and Petulius' susceptibility to the Siren's allure), while the concluding union between the nymphs and foresters is imposed, rather than achieved through service and devotion, violating audience expectation. Instead of closing with the establishment of a universal harmony at one with the concept of a golden age world (cf. the concluding scene of *As You Like It*), the play ends upon a note of discord (cf. Nisa's warning of her enduring coldness at 5.4.144–7), and with the suggestion of future infidelity (cf. Niobe's reiteration of her fickleness at 5.4.164–6). A dark shadow is thus cast across the Arcadian landscape, prompting reflection on the assumptions underpinning the genre (e.g. the life-enhancing nature of love) and complicating the application of the play to contemporary concerns (see pp. 29–34 below).

The kinds of pastoral entertainment offered to the sovereign both at court and during the royal progress, as the examples cited above suggest, were largely allegorical in mode and heavily reliant on the use of emblem. During the Queen's visit to the Earl of Hertford at Elvetham in 1591, for example, the stance of the monarch's host towards the exemplary virtue of his royal guest was expressed through a device involving six virgins 'remoouing blockes out of her maiesties way; which blocks were supposed to bee layde there by the person of *Enuie*, whose condition is, to enuie at euery good thing, but especially to malice the proceedings of *Vertue*, and the glory of true *Maiestie*'.[54] The popularity of such 'speaking pictures' is well attested throughout the early modern period,[55] and *Love's Metamorphosis*, like the majority of Lyly's plays, may be aligned with both contemporary court panegyric and the tastes of its era in its use of the projection of meaning through significant spectacle. In Act 1, for example, the attitudes of the three foresters are expressed by means of the 'scutcheons' which they hang on a tree dedicated to Ceres (cf. the type of courtly wooing enacted in *Pericles*, 2.2); while the characters of Nisa, Celia, and Niobe are defined through the flowers in the garlands which they hang on the same tree (cf. Perdita's distribution of flowers appropriate to the nature of their recipients in Act 4 of *The Winter's Tale*). The dancing and singing that take place in 1.2 around Ceres' tree denote the maidens' devotion to the virtue embodied in the goddess they serve, while Erisichthon's felling of the tree is symbolic of his blasphemous assertion of his authority over both the gods and the natural world. Similarly, the neoplatonic equation between monstrosity of form and nature (cf. Spenser's representation of moral qualities in *The Fairie Queene*) underlies the representation of the Siren, while the objects into which the recalcitrant nymphs are transformed as a punishment by Cupid are indicative of their inner selves. The use by the dramatist of an inherited stock of visual motifs serves to position the play within a network of allusions extending beyond the scope of the work, contributing to its location in a conceptual arena, removed from the specificities of a particular world.[56]

The timelessness of the action, promoted by the evocation of the pastoral world and the use of an inherited visual language, is further enforced by an insistent use of comparisons derived from received wisdom and the literary stock. The euphuistic mode, with which the Lylian corpus as a whole is inextricably associated, is noted for its illustrative analogies, turning, characteristically, upon the co-existence of contrasting properties in a single phenomenon, and drawn from proverbial lore, classical literature and mythology, and the more fabulous aspects of the natural world. In *The Anatomy of Wit*, for example, Euphues encourages himself in the pursuit of Lucilla with the recollection that 'fire cometh out of the hardest flint with the steel; oil out of the driest jet by the fire; love out of the stoniest heart by faith, by trust, by time. Had Tarquinius used his love with colours of continuance, Lucretia would either with some pity have answered his desire, or with some persuasion have stayed her death' (p. 57). Similarly, in *Love's Metamorphosis*, Silvestris reminds Niobe that 'Polypus . . . is ever of the colour of the stone it sticketh to', that 'a river running into divers brooks becometh shallow', and that 'Turtles flock by couples, and breed both joy and young ones', while Niobe counters that 'The oak findeth no fault with the dew because it also falleth on the bramble', and asks why 'had Argus an hundred eyes, and might have seen with one?' (3.1.85–111). While conforming to the paradigm of Lyly's prose and dramatic works, however, in its expansion of the arena of the action through its extensive use of figurative language, *Love's Metamorphosis* differs from the majority of the dramatist's compositions in the relatively narrow range of its classical allusions, comparatively slight reliance upon the fabulous, and marked dependence upon adage and proverb. The classical myths and references woven into the fabric of the play are largely Ovidian,[57] in keeping with the play's emphasis on transformation and its focus upon the nature of love (cf. the stories evoked by Fidelia at 1.2.118ff. and the mottoes hung by the foresters on Ceres' tree in Act 1);[58] and though such unfamiliar creatures as the polypus (3.1.85) and the salamich (3.1.142), and such exotic flowers as 'salmints' (1.2.5–6) inhabit the mental landscape of the dramatis personae, they occupy a world in which the bunting (cf. 1.2.36) and the dotterel (4.2.76), or the holly (1.2.9–11) and the nettle (3.2.74–7) are more readily encountered. At the same time, while proverbial utterances and stock comparisons position the speakers within a context of traditional moral assumptions, or inherited beliefs (cf. 'Cruelty is for tigers, pride for peacocks, inconstancy for fools': 5.1.60–1), contributing to the universality of the work, analogies more closely linked to sixteenth-century customs and social conditions endow the action with a degree of immediacy. Cupid alludes to the sixteenth-century use of flowers as personal adornments when he declares of Celia that, once transformed into a flower, 'men in the morning [shall] wear thee in their hats, and at night cast thee at their heels' (4.1.110–11); while Protea plays on the phrasing of usurers' bonds to express her distaste for the Merchant (3.2.50–4). The figurative language of the play thus evokes a universe that is simultaneously timeless and contemporary, familiar and remote,[59] combining with the use of Ovid, the pastoral mode, and the emblem tradition to produce a work wholly in tune with the cultural preferences of its age, while being removed, in its non-naturalistic mode, from the everyday.

STYLE AND STRUCTURE

'A model of symmetry',[60] *Love's Metamorphosis* is justly celebrated for the clarity and polish of its design. As in *Galatea*, to which the work, as noted above, is closely related, the action is set in a universe subject to change and organized around a conflict between love and chastity involving a challenge to the authority of the gods, but whereas in the earlier composition characters independent of the principal figures and extraneous to the amatory interest inhabit the world of the play, in *Love's Metamorphosis* all the dramatis personae are interdependent, and implicated in the exploration of the central themes (see p. 11 above). At the same time, the greater clarity of focus achieved through the shared concerns of the three strands of the plot is heightened by the process of simplification undergone by mortals and gods. Whereas in the earlier play the tension between love and chastity was partly enacted through the conflicting impulses of characters unexpectedly subject to love (cf. the opposing desires of Diana's nymphs), in *Love's Metamorphosis* the divided selves of the protagonists of the earlier play have given place to a kind of drama in which the stances of the figures are single and seemingly unchanging (cf. the foresters' pursuit of love), with oppositions defined through contrasting positions rather than through the doubts and uncertainties of specific individuals. The resolution achieved at the close of the play is consequently not the product of a process of experience (cf. the final commitment of Galatea and Phillida to one another that prompts the intervention of Venus in *Galatea*), but imposed by external agencies (cf. the marriages between the foresters and maidens ordained by Cupid in *Love's Metamorphosis*, 5.4), contributing to the patterned exploration of a concept (the multifaceted nature of love), rather than the simultaneous exhibition and enactment of a complex state.

It is upon the close correspondence between style and structure, however, that the claim that *Love's Metamorphosis* represents the high-water mark of one aspect of Lyly's art principally rests. In common with Lylian comedy as a whole, the long set-piece speeches of the drama exhibit the syntactic and syllabic patterning, antithetical balance (frequently pointed by assonance or alliteration), wordplay, and use of analogies turning upon the fusion of contrasting properties in a single phenomenon, or illustrative of a universal susceptibility to change, characteristic of euphuistic prose.[61] The devices are drawn together in the speech of the dying Fidelia, who ends her life with the following adieu to her own sex: 'Farewell, ladies, whose lives are subject to many mischiefs; for if you be fair, it is hard to be chaste, if chaste, impossible to be safe. If you be young, you will quickly bend; if bend, you are suddenly broken. If you be foul, you shall seldom be flattered; if you be not flattered, you will ever be sorrowful. Beauty is a firm fickleness, youth a feeble stayedness, deformity a continual sadness' (1.2.147–54).

It is not merely the more lengthy speeches of the drama, however, that exhibit the typical features of the style. As in all Lyly's plays, the dialogue as a whole combines to develop a widening circle of ambivalence, which expands from the single word, which is found to be capable of more than one meaning, through antithetically constructed statements, supported by analogies which themselves turn on some species of 'doubleness',[62] to the enunciation of linguistically parallel but opposing positions which preclude any sense of finality or closure. In 3.2, for example, Protea and the Merchant have the following exchange (lines 70–9):

> *Merchant.* You are now mine, Protea.
> *Protea.* And mine own.
> *Merchant.* In will, not power.
> *Protea.* In power, if I will.
> *Merchant.* I perceive nettles, gently touched, sting; but,
>   roughly handled, make no smart.
> *Protea.* Yet, roughly handled, nettles are nettles; and a wasp
>   is a wasp, though she lose her sting.
> *Merchant.* But then they do no harm.
> *Protea.* Nor good.

The non-naturalistic, seesaw oppositions of the dialogue, heightened in this instance by the use of stichomythia,[63] encourage an awareness on the part of the audience of artifice or design, and the sense of patterning is further promoted by the serial listing of parallel propositions, which suggest the universality, or widen the application, of the speakers' positions. Just as Fidelia laments, for example, in the speech quoted above, that, 'Beauty is a firm fickleness, youth a feeble stayedness, deformity a continual sadness' (1.2.153–4), so Erisichthon affirms that 'It is not your fair faces as smooth as jet, nor your enticing eyes though they drew iron like adamants, nor your filed speeches were they as forcible as Thessalides', that shall make me any way flexible' (1.2.73–7), while Nisa declares that Erisichthon will be subject to Ceres' revenge 'If there be power in her deity, in her mind pity, or virtue in virginity' (1.2.172–3). The triplets contribute, through their simultaneous similarity and dissimilarity, to the creation of a montage of oppositions, with every proposition subject to qualification through the exhibition of alternative potentialities or fresh applications, and the insistent analogical emphasis on change. The components of the dramatic language thus combine, paradoxically, to enable both the precise articulation of immutable positions (e.g. hostility or commitment to love) and the projection of a radically unstable intellectual and physical milieu, in which everything is capable of modification, and nothing is absolute, including the polarized concepts to which the speakers refer.

The action of *Love's Metamorphosis* is similarly structured upon parallelism and contrast.[64] At the outset of the play, three young men express, sequentially, their love for three nymphs dedicated to chastity, and hang tokens expressive of their passion on a tree dedicated to Ceres; while in the following scene, which functions as a mirror image of the first, three young women announce, in sequence, their opposition to love and devotion to Ceres, and deride the mottoes left on the tree by the lovers. The straightforward oppositions set up here between men and maidens, love and chastity, are then complicated by the entrance of Erisichthon, who parallels the lovers in his masculinity, but is old rather than young, and corresponds to the maidens in being hostile to affection, but is antagonistic rather than deferential to Ceres. The acts of devotion conducted around Ceres' tree by the youthful characters are counterpointed by the act of desecration that the mature Erisichthon performs, while the tree, which has formed the focal point of the two opening scenes, exhibits the duality informing the imagery throughout, in that it proves, at the close of the act, to enclose the person of a nymph, and to be capable of both feeling and speech.[65]

The oppositions set up in the opening scenes of the drama are further expanded as the action evolves. In Act 2, for example, the attitudes of the men and maidens are qualified and placed in a larger context through an encounter between the deities who embody their contrasting positions, while the multifaceted nature of amatory experience is further anatomized, as the drama unfolds, through a series of fresh juxtapositions. The self-centred passion of the foresters, for example, which admits the transformation of their intransigent mistresses into subhuman form, is contrasted with the selfless love of Protea who is ready to be changed into 'a bird, hare, or lamb' (3.2.34) to promote the welfare of her self-regarding father. Similarly the chastity of Fidelia, who is arborified to avoid lust, is set against the destructive sexuality of the Siren, who seeks to arouse it, while the inconstancy of Petulius in the face of temptation is contrasted with Protea's unswerving devotion. The initial univocality of the foresters is destabilized once their mistresses are returned to their human shapes (e.g. by Ramis' rejection of Silvestris' assertion that love is worthless if enforced: 5.3.14–22); while the divergent attitudes of the three maidens, together with the stances of Ceres and Fidelia, exhibit the range of considerations and motives comprehended within the repudiation of love.

Just as the balanced oppositions of the euphuistic mode are enacted through the antithetical organization of character and scene, so the sense of fluidity promoted through the insistent use of analogies turning upon duality and change has its equivalent in the metamorphoses enacted in the course of the drama. The tree that occupies a central position in the opening scene, for example, was once a nymph devoted to Ceres, while Nisa, Celia, and Niobe are transformed in the course of the action into a rock, a flower, and a bird. Protea becomes a fisherman through the agency of Neptune, and then assumes the shape of Ulysses to rescue her lover from the wiles of the Siren, and Erisichthon is radically changed through the action of Famine before being returned by Ceres to 'his former state' (5.4.16). Similarly, the pervasive ambiguity promoted through the imagery (cf. 'Fresh flowers have crooked roots': 3.1.55) has its visual counterpart in the 'doubleness' of the dramatis personae, most notably that of the Siren, 'who only hath the voice and face of a virgin, the rest all fish, and feathers, and filth' (4.2.103–4), and the aged Ulysses, whose 'crooked age' (4.2.82) gives way to the form of a young woman.

The use of triplets, which constitutes, as noted above, a further feature of the style also has its counterpart in the structuring of the work. Just as propositions are illustrated through an assemblage of parallel instances, so the oppositions explored in the course of the action are defined through trios of comparable states. In the opening scene of the play, for example, the predicament of one lover is echoed in those of two more (cf. '*Montanus.* I love a nymph that mocks love. / *Ramis.* And I one that hates love. / *Silvestris.* I one that thinks herself above love': 1.1.26–9), and the process of 'numbering down the line',[66] through which the simultaneous likeness and dissimilarity of their situations is conveyed, is characteristic of both their exchanges with one another and their responses to the questions posed by Cupid (cf. '*Ramis.* Mine most cruel, which she calleth constancy. / *Montanus.* Mine most fair, but most proud. / *Silvestris.* Mine most witty, but most wavering': 4.1.42–5). In the same way, three maidens, rather than one, repudiate the amatory state, are equally obdurate when instructed to yield to the judgement of Cupid (cf. '*Nisa.* Not I! / *Niobe.* Nor I! / *Celia.* Nor I!': 5.4.60–2), and incredulous at being required to marry those who brought about their physical change (cf. '*Nisa.* Shall I yield to him that practised my destruction . . . / *Celia.* Shall I yield to him that made so small account of my beauty . . . / *Niobe.* Shall I yield to him that caused me have wings . . . ?': 5.4.122–36).[67] The sequential enunciation of parallel positions, initiated at the start of the play, is developed, moreover, as the action evolves, into the serial entrances of comparable groups, contributing to the sense of artifice, or scheme, promoted by the drama as a whole. In 3.1, for example, the three pairs of lovers enter and exit in turn, with each forester pursuing his fleeing mistress, pleading his cause, and being scornfully rejected by her, before the men reassemble at the close, to exclaim in sequence on the maidens' defects.[68] The process of coming together, performing a sequence of exchanges, and moving apart, invites an association with dance,[69] and the scene is overtly linked with other types of three-part musical composition by a play on 'bass', 'mean', and 'treble' in the exchange between Niobe and Silvestris (3.1.131–8).[70] Just as Niobe's heart-strings are 'double and treble' (3.1.137), so too is the idiom of her world, and the organization of the incidents in which she participates, and the dramatic arena to which she belongs.

The integral relationship between the style and structure of the drama gives rise to an ever-expanding pattern of oppositions, which constitutes an ideal vehicle for the exploration of a multifaceted state. Just as Lyly's earliest work announces itself as an 'anatomy of wit', so *Love's Metamorphosis* might be said to be an anatomy of love, unfolding, with quasi-scientific precision, the intricate tissue of impulses informing a complex condition. At the same time, however, the play's systematic exhibition of alternative potentialities leads, in a typically Lylian paradox, not towards a final definition of the erotic impulse but away from an ultimate understanding into a 'labyrinth of conceits'.[71] Just as the single word proves, in the course of the drama, to be unexpectedly ambiguous, so the nature of love proves elusive, emerging, like every component of the Lylian universe, to be subject to infinite qualification.[72]

LOVE AND METAMORPHOSIS

Like so many other aspects of the work, the title of *Love's Metamorphosis* proves capable of yielding 'divers significations'.[73] Whereas on the one hand it might be understood as referring to the changes brought about by Love (i.e. Cupid) in the course of the play, such as the transformation of Nisa, Celia, and Niobe into a rock, a flower, and a bird, on the other it might point to the mutations to which love itself is subject, as seen, for example, in the vengeful stances adopted by the three foresters towards the nymphs of Ceres who decline to yield to their suits. Its thrust is further complicated, moreover, by the intertextual relationships set up in the course of the work, with a number of references alluding to the contrast between the Cupid of this play and the 'little god' of the dramatist's previous compositions, inviting reflection on the significance of the metamorphosis that the play's presiding deity has himself undergone. The fact that other agencies are also productive of change (e.g. Ceres, who transforms Erisichthon through hunger, and Neptune, who enables the transformation of Protea) adds a further layer of uncertainty, promoting awareness of the difference between the kinds of metamorphosis instigated by Cupid and those engineered by other powers. At the same time, the ambiguity of the formulation is heightened by the complex nature of the amatory state, which is shown in the course of the drama to evade straightforward definition, embracing a spectrum of stances ranging from lust to self-sacrificing devotion, and to be capable of construction as both cruel and benign.

The play opens with a debate between three foresters over whether love may be said to be all-pervasive, in view of the lack of affection in the world; and whether it may be said to be spiritual, given that its object is the satisfaction of a physical desire. The arguments advanced here might be said to be blasphemous in that they call in question the supremacy of Cupid, and the subsequent action explores the validity of the speakers' positions. For all their doubts about the nature of love, the three men declare their devotion to three nymphs dedicated to the service of Ceres, each of whom embodies one aspect of the conventional Petrarchan mistress, in that they are (from the perspective of their lovers) cruel, coy, and inconstant. The seemingly uncomplicated opposition set up here between deserving lover and unkind lady is qualified in the scene that follows in which the maidens are first introduced. While their scorn of love conforms to their initial characterization, the fact that they define themselves as followers of Ceres, goddess of chastity, permits their repudiation of love to be seen as a virtue, rather than a vice, and this view of their position is further promoted by the account that the arborified Fidelia, herself once a follower of Ceres, offers of the process that leads to her death. Fleeing from the lust of a satyr, prior to the opening of the play, she was transformed by the gods into inanimate form, and laments the ambivalence of both men and deities towards the virtue she has sought to uphold (cf. 'there is nothing more hateful than to be chaste, whose bodies are followed in the world with lust, and prosecuted in the graves with tyranny . . . What is that chastity which so few women study to keep, and both gods and men seek to violate? If only a naked name, why are we so superstitious of a hollow sound? If a rare virtue, why are men

so careless of an exceeding rareness?': 1.2.127–38). Her fate in the
course of the drama lends weight, moreover, to the emerging definition of love as physical and destructive, rather than spiritual and
creative, and thus to the stance towards masculine desire adopted
by the nymphs. The assault that she suffers at the hands of Erisichthon is equated with rape in her dying speech, and the association
is heightened by the stress laid in the course of the scene on the
shedding of virgin blood, and the challenge that her fate offers to
Ceres (cf. 'If Ceres seek no revenge, then let virginity be not only
the scorn of savage people, but the spoil': 1.2.144–6).

In characteristically Lylian fashion, however, the oppositions set
up in the opening act of the drama are progressively destabilized as
the action evolves.[74] The choice of Ceres (conventionally figured as
the goddess of the harvest and thus associated with fertility) as the
divine embodiment of chastity is a surprising one, running counter
to the classical tradition, and the position adopted by the deity in
the following act fails to conform to the expectations aroused in the
course of the opening scenes. Though she deplores the fate of
Fidelia, and seeks revenge on Erisichthon for his sacrilegious act,
she warns her followers against their arrogant stance towards Cupid,
and herself makes offerings to him in acknowledgement of his power
(compare the very different stance of Diana towards Venus in
Galatea, in which the deities remain bitterly opposed to one another
throughout). At the same time, Cupid himself accords with neither
the wayward child of Lyly's earlier plays nor the uncompromising
opponent of chastity that the first act encourages the spectator to
expect. Rather than promoting sexual desire, he denies that 'lust
followeth love' (2.1.138), asserting not the primacy of the amatory
instinct over the virtue that Ceres embodies but the falsity of the
distinction between the two (cf. 'lovers are chaste! For what is love,
divine love, but the quintessence of chastity' (2.1.139–40).

While the encounter between Cupid and Ceres in Act 2 serves to
distinguish love from lust, and to align it with chastity, it simultaneously instigates a divorce between chastity and virginity (cf. 'lovers
are chaste') that reflects back on the stances of the maidens in the
opening scene. The imagery through which the nymphs define their
repudiation of love carries associations of sterility, and suggests the
emaciation of the physical self (cf. 'I am content to wither before I
be worn, and deprive myself of that which so many desire': 1.2.14–
16), forging an unexpected link between the fate that they embrace
and that imposed on Erisichthon by Ceres.[75] Their hostility to men,

reiterated at the start of 3.1, looks forward to the position of the Siren, who appears in the following act, and who functions as their polar opposite in that she invites rather than repudiates amatory desire, but whose mirror is reflective of her similarly self-enclosed state. The misogynistic attitudes of both nymphs and Siren stand in sharp contrast, moreover, to the stance of Erisichthon's daughter, Protea, who is warm in her approval of men (cf. 4.2.29–30), and whose capacity to feed her father, and to save her lover from the Siren's wiles, is directly linked to her seduction by Neptune. The traditional opposition between love and chastity advanced at the outset of the play has thus given place by this stage of the drama to a much more complex set of antithetical positions, which serve to divorce not only chastity from virginity but, more surprisingly perhaps, virginity from virtue.

While the unyielding self-sufficiency of the virgin state becomes more problematic in the course of the work, so too does the amatory condition that it is conventionally taken to oppose. Whereas, at the beginning of the play, the foresters' love for the nymphs appears to stand in opposition to the lust of the satyr who pursued Fidelia, and the sexual violence and exploitation implicit in Erisichthon's assault upon Ceres' tree and subsequent sale of his daughter to the Merchant, the attitudes of the male figures are increasingly elided when the maidens continue to resist their lovers' suits. The revenges proposed by the foresters, and declared by Cupid to be 'reasonable' (4.1.99), admit the transformation of the loved one into subhuman form (cf. the fate of Fidelia), while the accommodation achieved at the close of the play involves the nymphs' submission to their lovers' desires not through choice or persuasion but threat (cf. 'if they yield not I will turn them again: not to flowers, or stones, or birds, but to monsters, no less filthy to be seen than to be named hateful': 5.4.114–16). The cruelty of Cupid's power is increasingly stressed, moreover, as the action evolves, not merely by those wedded to virginity but by the embodiment of the amatory instinct himself. Though Fidelia's contention that Erisichthon's assault upon her translated body is a product of Cupid's 'spite' at her 'unspotted mind' (1.2.109–10) is countered by the deity's emphatic repudiation of lust, the irresistibility and pain of the amatory state are both repeatedly asserted and displayed. Ceres' angry protest at the treatment of her nymphs, for example, is answered by Cupid's arbitrary, 'sic volo, sic iubeo' ('Thus I wish, thus I command': 5.1.7), while her question, 'Art thou so cruel?', in response to his assertion of the extent of his power, receives the uncompromising answer, 'To those that resist, a lion; to those that submit, a lamb' (5.1.23–5). Though Silvestris has some reservations about possessing a mistress whose love is the product of enforcement (cf. 'what joy can there be in our lives, or in our loves sweetness, when every kiss shall be sealed with a curse, and every kind word proceed of fear, not affection?': 5.3.15–18), Ramis brushes his inhibitions aside (cf. 'Let them curse all day, so I may have but one kiss at night': 5.3.21–2), and later expresses his joy at his union with a mistress who has been compelled by Cupid to accede to his desires, and who warns him that he might well find her 'cold in love' (5.4.144–5). The servant / mistress roles of the Petrarchan relationship are thus reversed by the close of the play, in a denouement that rests upon the achievement of love, not through the exhibition of desert (cf. Eumenides' achievement of the reluctant Semele in *Endymion*) but on power.

While the pitilessness of Love (cf. 'To those that resist, a lion') is exhibited through the fate of Ceres' nymphs, his benign aspect (cf. 'to those that submit, a lamb') is displayed through the figure of Erisichthon's daughter, Protea. Though, from one perspective, the experience of the play's virgins might be said to exhibit the cruelty of the amatory instinct, from another it may be seen as a representation of the ultimately beneficial process through which maiden inhibition is overcome – and Protea's experience offers an example of the life-enhancing consequences of sexual surrender. Having yielded to the amorous advances of Neptune, she is enabled, through his patronage, to feed her undeserving father, who is ready to sell her into probable prostitution to save his life, and to rescue her erring lover from the lust embodied in the Siren, and it is her 'faithful love' (5.4.27) that prompts Cupid to restore the nymphs to human form and release Erisichthon from the punishment imposed by Ceres. The universal 'kindness' (5.4.197) with which the play concludes is thus a direct consequence of her openness to the emotion that Ceres' followers reject, while the distance between the self-centred desires of the foresters and her unselfregarding devotion to others bears witness to the validity of Cupid's assertion that the spectrum of love embraces a range of conditions, 'as much as between sickness and health, though in both be life' (5.1.28–9).

The ambiguity of the emotion that the play's supreme deity embodies does not solely reside, however, in the divergent types of behaviour to which the amatory instinct gives rise. At the outset of the play the foresters cast doubt on both the spirituality and pervasiveness of love, and thus on the extent of Cupid's power. In the course of the drama, however, Cupid asserts not only his authority over Ceres but his pre-eminence among the gods as a whole, declaring that he is 'such a god as maketh thunder fall out of Jove's hand by throwing thoughts into his heart, and to be more terrified with the sparkling of a lady's eye than men with the flashes of his lightning; such a god that hath kindled more fire in Neptune's bosom than the whole sea which he is king of can quench', who has 'Such power . . . that Pluto's never-dying fire doth but scorch in respect of [his] flames', and who has stirred amatory feelings in Diana and Vesta (5.1.14–21). Ceres' deference towards him substantiates his position of authority in the play world, while his closing speech to the lovers emphasizes the spiritual nature of the relationships he has instigated through his stress on the need for them to 'sacrifice vows' before giving way to desire (5.4.181–3). At the same time, however, aspects of the drama run counter to his assertion of his supremacy over gods and humanity, undermining the spirituality of the emotion he instils. Though he is capable of influencing the conduct of his fellow deities, he is also dependent upon them, as he himself admits (cf. *'sine Cerere et Baccho friget Venus'*: 5.1.53), while there is some indication that although he has absolute, if unselective, power over hearts (cf. 'shooting every minute a thousand shafts, I know not on whose heart they light': 4.1.39–40), he is not capable of controlling minds. His position of authority in relation to the three nymphs is comparable in some respects to that of the Merchant in relation to Protea, and it is made clear in the course of the action that, though the Merchant is in a position to exert his will over the latter's physical self, he cannot control every aspect of her being (cf. *'Merchant.* You are now mine, Protea. / *Protea.* And mine own. / *Merchant.* In will, not power. / *Protea.* In power, if I will': 3.2.70–3). Similarly, though Cupid is able to metamorphose the nymphs when they resist his authority, his transformatory power does not extend to their minds, in that they decline to accede to their lovers when returned to human form, and submit only when subject to threat. The nymphs maintain, moreover, that their former attitudes will be carried forward into their conduct as wives (5.4.144–66), and though Cupid declares at the close of the play that he will 'make such unspotted loves among you that there shall be no suspicion nor jar, no unkindness nor jealousy' (5.4.174–6), his ability to fulfil that promise is untested, and must thus remain open to doubt.

The metamorphoses that the audience's understanding of the nature of love undergoes in the course of the work have given rise to considerable academic disagreement over both the tone of the drama and its ultimate thrust. Though it is generally agreed that the play offers an anatomy of love, exhibiting a spectrum of attitudes to the sexual impulse,[76] the degree to which a final definition is achieved at the close remains a matter of dispute. Bond, for example, sees the denouement of the play as similar to that of *Galatea*, in that 'both celebrate the triumph of true love over a false ideal of chastity which declines and mocks at marriage',[77] while Saccio, who also sees the outcome of the action as celebratory, argues that 'this gallery . . . is not merely a showcase of loves. It is part of the unfolding of the central image of Cupid [who] . . . comes to represent love in the Neoplatonic sense initially doubted by the foresters: love as that which orders and preserves the world, whose power is absolute, and whose realm is everywhere.'[78] Similarly, though he stresses the material rather than the spiritual, Dooley maintains that the play moves towards a positive conclusion, exhibiting 'the material and emotional requirements that were perceived to be necessary for a healthy mind and body and thus for a healthy, well-ordered body politic in the early modern period'.[79] For other critics, however, the play is far more open-ended. Edge notes that 'at least three different views' may be taken of the accommodation achieved in the final scene, ranging from 'a fanciful triumph of love over obstacles' to a synthesis fraught with contradictions, implying that the play's 'debates will begin anew';[80] while for Daniel the play is 'a Breughel-like tapestry of the unresolved dilemmas of humankind', which 'leaves everything unresolved at the end'.[81] At a further extreme from the positions adopted by Bond and Saccio, Pincombe sees the deity constructed by the latter as the embodiment of the Neoplatonic ideal in wholly negative terms (cf. 'Cupid turns out to be just as tyrannical as all the other gods in Lyly's plays: cross him, and he will threaten violence'), maintaining that he cannot 'be identified with *eros*', in that 'he cannot instil love in the hearts of the nymphs'.[82] Similarly Lancashire argues that the finale 'is no real victory for love', and though the drama may be read as a 'psychological allegory [with] the nymphs overcoming immature desires for virginity through fear of being unnatural', the effect overall 'is strongly negative or ironic'.[83] And whereas for Houppert the drama is simply 'an erotic intrigue leading to sexual fulfillment' and is thus 'one of the most universal of Lyly's plays',[84] for Parnell it resists 'sober, formal analysis' requiring to be read 'with an unpedantic and slightly wayward imagination'.[85]

It is a character within the drama, however, who supplies the most intriguing reading of the work. Lylian comedy as a whole is insistently self-referential, and the plays are frequently furnished with prologues and epilogues which assert the resistance of the material to final analysis and the role played by the spectator in the assignment of meaning. The epilogue to *Sappho and Phao*, for example, describes the play as 'a labyrinth of conceits' (line 3), while the prologue for a court performance of *Campaspe* likens the drama to 'the dancing of Agrippa his shadows, who in the moment they were seen were of any shape one would conceive' (lines 13–15). Though the extant text of *Love's Metamorphosis* lacks the framing devices characteristic of Lyly's plays,[86] a commentary is supplied on the action through an exchange in the final act. At the close of the encounter between Petulius and the Siren in 4.2, Protea promises to tell her lover the history of her life, comprising, as the audience is later informed, much of the matter of the play (cf. 'I have told both my father's misfortunes, grown by stoutness, and mine, by weakness; his thwarting of Ceres, my yielding to Neptune': 5.2.4–6). The second scene of Act 5 opens with Petulius' reflections on the story he has heard, and his comments offer a perspective on the events of the play as a whole: 'A strange discourse, Protea, by which I find the gods amorous, and virgins immortal; goddesses full of cruelty, and men of unhappiness' (5.2.1–3). The summary precedes the accommodation by Cupid achieved in the closing scene, and thus the 'kindness' (5.4.197) on which the play comes, in Erisichthon's view, to a close, but it is indicative, nevertheless, of the distance between the nature of the universe in which the drama is set and the golden world of the pastoral ideal. For all the elegance of its plotting, *Love's Metamorphosis* is indeed a 'strange discourse', and its emphasis upon cruelty and unhappiness has given rise to a further source of scholarly disagreement – the nature and extent of its application to the concerns of the late sixteenth-century court.

GENDER POLITICS AND THE ELIZABETHAN COURT

Though there is no surviving record of a production of *Love's Metamorphosis* at court, there is considerable evidence to suggest that the play was designed for performance before the Queen. The title-page of the 1601 quarto describes the work as a 'Courtly Pastorall', and the choice of mode confirms the implication that the drama was written for an aristocratic audience (see pp. 12–13 above). The play pointedly locates itself, as noted above, within a sequence of works designed for the monarch's entertainment, and the title-page of the quarto indicates that it was written for the same troupe (the Children of Paul's) that had performed the two preceding plays in the group. The central concern of the work is also indicative that the play was written with the sovereign in mind. The tension between love and chastity is a recurring theme of both Lylian comedy and Elizabethan court panegyric as a whole, reflecting upon the transcendent virtue of a monarch superior to fleshly desires.[87]

While the proposition that the play was written for a courtly audience is relatively easy to substantiate, however, the extent of its engagement with contemporary issues is far more difficult to assess. It is generally agreed that, for all their evasive character, the majority of Lyly's comedies celebrate the head of state to some degree, in both her public and private aspects, and that figures equatable in some measure with the sovereign are identifiable in the plays. The situation of the queen of *Sappho and Phao*, for example, who subjugates her private desires to the interests of the state, is universally agreed to reflect upon that of Elizabeth in her role as the Virgin Queen, while the exemplary prince who stands in opposition to the deluded King of Phrygia in *Midas* is unequivocally associated with the divinely-ordained sovereign who united the realm against Philip II of Spain (see *Midas*, 3.1.1–72). In the case of *Love's Metamorphosis*, however, such parallels are much more difficult to adduce, and commentators are consequently divided over the extent to which the work may be constructed as a comment on late sixteenth-century affairs. While Bond, for example, at one extreme, sees the piece as a political allegory, in which Lyly represents 'in the churlish farmer, Erisichthon, who owes his wealth to Ceres' bounty, the ungrateful designs of the favourite Essex against his royal mistress',[88] Hunter argues, at the other, that the events of the play 'cannot be plausibly translated into happenings in the court of Elizabeth', and that 'it is difficult to find evidence . . . of any intention to depict the Queen'.[89] The pursuit of the kind of one-to-one parallels proposed by Bond between the plot of the play and sixteenth-century political events has been largely discredited in recent times, but it is nevertheless difficult to endorse the proposition that the drama has no bearing upon the audience to which it was initially addressed. The concern with love and chastity, the references to earlier works more overtly directed towards their principal spectator, and the inclusion, in the person of Ceres, of a female authority figure comparable with those more readily equatable with the monarch elsewhere in the Lylian corpus (cf. Sappho in *Sappho and Phao*, and Cynthia in *Endymion*) all invite association with the allusive mode of Lylian court comedy as a whole, and the application of the work to events beyond the play world. At the same time, however, neither the relationship between love and chastity presented in the course of the drama nor the role assigned to the principal representative of the latter corresponds with that of earlier plays.[90] Whereas chastity triumphs over love in *Sappho and Phao*, signalled by the Queen's appropriation of Cupid and defeat of Venus, while the chief representative of virginity in *Galatea* achieves a species of truce with the representatives of love, in *Love's Metamorphosis* virginity is distinguished from chastity, the distinction between love and chastity is shown to be a false one, and the embodiment of the unsullied female state concedes the necessity to yield to Cupid's commands (see p. 23 above). Rather than celebrating the supreme virtue of a monarch superior to earthly desires, the play may thus be seen as an exploration of the concepts underpinning the cult of Elizabeth as a whole (e.g. the equation between virginity and virtue); and its pointed differentiation between chastity and celibacy, and assertion of the compatibility of the former with marital love, may well reflect growing anxiety in the closing decades of the sixteenth century regarding the implications of the Queen's unmarried state.

Some support for the contention that the play is indicative of the gathering concern evident in the late Tudor period for the future of the realm may be found in the 'Glass for Europe' with which *Euphues and His England* concludes. The closing encomium upon the supreme virtue of the sovereign ends with the wish that 'as she hath lived forty years a virgin in great majesty, so she may live fourscore years a mother with great joy, that as with her we have long time had peace and plenty, so by her we may ever have quietness and abundance; wishing this, even from the bottom of a heart that wisheth well to England, though feareth ill, that either the world may end before she die or she live to see her children's children in the world'.[91] The passage appears to reflect uncertainty on Lyly's part with regard to the Queen's age, in that Elizabeth was fortyseven, rather than forty when the work was composed,[92] and the argument that *Love's Metamorphosis* also reflects public anxiety at the monarch's failure to supply the kingdom with an heir similarly depends upon chronological uncertainties of a variety of kinds. No agreement exists, as noted above, on the date of the play itself, and though its close relationship with *Galatea* admits composition as early as 1584–85, the possibility of a fruitful royal marriage at that time would have been viable only if Elizabeth had indeed been in her mid-forties, as Lyly appears to have supposed.[93]

Though the play's stance towards love and chastity may be linked, somewhat tentatively, with that of the party concerned to promote a royal marriage, the play is far from endorsing the misogynistic assumptions implicit in the notion of the 'monstrous regiment of women'. The drama insistently challenges the suppositions underpinning sixteenth-century gender relations, courting the approval of the audience to which it was initially addressed through a critique of the sexual mores of the age. Like the majority of items in the Lylian canon, the work has a predominance of female roles, and the positions adopted by the dramatis personae are strikingly at odds with patriarchal expectations. While the male characters are largely oppressive, irrational, exploitative, or weak, their female counterparts exhibit little respect for male authority, and are afforded the space to advance their own views. Erisichthon, for example, assaults Fidelia in an act that echoes the rape attempted upon her by a satyr prior to the opening of the play; Ramis, Montanus, and Silvestris, having been repudiated by the nymphs, pursue a self-defeating revenge upon those they profess to love; Erisichthon, rather than protecting his daughter as parental obligation dictates, is willing to sell her to save his own life; while the seemingly devoted lover, Petulius, quickly succumbs to the allure of the Siren. At the same time, the female characters develop a cogent counter-argument to the assumed necessity for women to conform to masculine desires. Fidelia, for example, dilates upon the double standards by which men simultaneously celebrate chastity and pursue its violation (1.2.107–38); Niobe asserts female rationality in arguing that to love at another's behest 'were to pull the brains out of my head' (3.1.94–5);[94] while Protea echoes the resolute Timoclea in *Campaspe* in her insistence to the Merchant that though the body may become the object of a male exchange, the will can not be similarly possessed (cf. *Love's Metamorphosis*, 3.2.70–9, and *Campaspe*, 1.1.50–6). It is in the closing scene of the drama, however, that patriarchal assumptions are most pointedly overturned. Having been transformed to subhuman forms for resisting the dictates of Cupid, the nymphs are restored through the agency of Ceres, who releases Erisichthon from the punishment she has imposed on him for the death of Fidelia and the violation of her grove, and promises that her followers will accede to the foresters' suits (cf. 'Cupid, here is Erisichthon in his former state; restore my nymphs to theirs. Then shall they embrace these lovers, who wither out their youth': 5.4.16–18). Both the expectations of those within the play world and the assumptions generated by the comic form encourage the audience to assume that the maidens will rejoice at their return to human shape, acknowledge their errors, and embrace the lovers who have pursued them throughout, permitting the play to conclude on a conventionally harmonious note, in accordance with social norms. To the surprise of those both inside and outside the play world, however, the nymphs emphatically decline to co-operate with Cupid's designs, and the terms in which they reject them command, equally surprisingly, a measure of respect. Nisa asserts that her impervious state was preferable to being 'dulled with the importunities of men, whose open flatteries make way to their secret lusts, retaining as little truth in their hearts as modesty in their words' (5.4.75–7); Celia questions the assumption that women should 'yield' to men because they 'say they love', as if 'our hearts were tied to their tongues and we must choose them by appointment, ourselves feeling no affection, and so have our thoughts bound prentices to their words' (5.4.93–8); while Niobe declares the air to be 'more constant than men's words' and repudiates the 'disorderly' nature of earthly love (5.4.103 and 107). Rather than complying, moreover, when further threatened by Cupid, they continue to question why they should yield, and again their objections to their suitors are not without force. Nisa asks why she should give herself to one 'that practised [her] destruction' (5.4.122), Celia queries why she should take one who 'made so small account of [her] beauty that he studied how he might never behold it again' (5.4.129–31), while Niobe questions why she should yield to one who 'caused me have wings, that I might fly farther from him' (5.4.136–7). Though constructed by Cupid as perversity, their refusal to capitulate to their lovers' desires may be seen as an entirely rational response to their experience in the course of the play, and the specious justifications offered by the foresters for their conduct fail to qualify the uneasiness of pairings finally achieved at the close by dictate – arguably interrogating the assumed propriety of female deference to the male will.[95]

Though, in theatrical terms, however, the nymphs' refusal to bow to Cupid's judgement constitutes the most surprising moment in the play, it is the role of Protea, rather than the obduracy of Nisa, Celia, or Niobe which offers the greatest challenge to sixteenth-century constructions of gender. The figure has its origins in Erisichthon's unnamed daughter in the Ovidian source, but is developed by the dramatist into a highly original creation.[96] Faithful to her erring lover, Petulius, and loyal to her unnatural father, for whom she is willing to be repeatedly sold, she appears at first glance to conform to the sixteenth-century ideal of the virtuous woman, deferential to the male will and ready to sacrifice herself on others' behalf. In one major respect, however, she departs from the conventional model of exemplary female behaviour, in that though still unmarried she is no longer a virgin. Seduced by Neptune prior to the opening of the play, she is able to feed her father and save her lover from the wiles of the Siren solely through the fulfilment of a promise made to her in the heat of passion by an amorous god, and the terms in which she prays for her seducer's assistance indicate no sense of resentment or betrayal at the loss of her virgin state (cf. 'Sacred Neptune, whose godhead conquered my maidenhead, be as ready to hear my passions as I was to believe thine, and perform that now, I entreat, which thou didst promise when thyself didst love': 3.2.27–30). Her seduction by Neptune is the more significant, moreover, in that it constitutes a departure by the dramatist from his source,[97] in which her unnamed counterpart is the victim of an act of rape, and thus exculpated from any complicity in her deflowerment. Nevertheless, for all her acquiescence in her sexual initiation, Protea is far from being an unsympathetic figure,[98] and is not disgraced by her actions but empowered. Petulius merely reflects on hearing her history, that 'hard iron falling into fire waxeth soft, and then the tender heart of a virgin, being in love, must needs melt' (5.2.7–9), while it is through the promise made to her by Neptune that she is able to fulfil her patriarchal obligations, evade the defilement threatened by her sale to the Merchant, and preserve her lover from the danger posed by the Siren. It is her 'faithful love' for Erisichthon, moreover, that moves Cupid 'to grant her desires, and to release [her father's] punishments' (5.4.27–9), facilitating the wider reconciliation achieved at the close. Neither chaste, silent (cf. her contemptuous exchange with the Merchant), nor conventionally obedient (in that she plans to circumvent her father's designs, and to save him by her own means), she violates all three major sixteenth-century assumptions regarding the nature of exemplary womanhood, but is nevertheless constructed by the dramatist as both virtuous and a force for good, emerging as the strongest, most clear-sighted, and sympathetic woman in the play.

While the play's critique of virginity may thus be aligned with contemporary political concerns, its representation of male / female relationships registers a keen awareness, highly relevant to the Elizabethan court, of the problematic nature of a social model based upon the assumed propriety of female subjection. Though virginity is distinguished from chastity, allowing for the reconciliation of the Queen's unsullied state with a royal marriage, and loss of virginity is shown as potentially empowering, the play is far from exhibiting unqualified disenchantment with the cult of the Virgin Queen, in that none of the courses available to the female characters is wholly desirable, while the public good (as perceived by the play's authority figures) is not achieved without private cost. Rather than documenting the growth of the playwright's 'resistance to Eliza', as Pincombe suggests,[99] the drama is elegantly evasive, like Lylian comedy as a whole, neither advocating nor repudiating a particular path, but leading the audience, as in *Sappho and Phao*, through a 'labyrinth of conceits'[100] designed to exhibit the complex nature of socio-sexual interactions before leaving them to ponder, as the barely reconciled lovers leave the stage together at the close, whether it is indeed 'As good', as Montanus asserts, to 'yield . . . submissively, and satisfy part of our affections' (1.1.24–5), or better to remain aloof from the amatory sphere, as Nisa claims, and to show 'discretion' (3.1.29).

DRAMATURGY, STAGING, AND THE STAGE HISTORY OF THE PLAY

A 'courtly pastoral', *Love's Metamorphosis* evokes, like the majority of Lyly's plays, a world remote from day-to-day experience.[101] The locations, divorced from any specific temporal reality (e.g. a grove, a sea-shore), the names of the characters, which look back to classical myth (e.g. Niobe, Erisichthon), the inclusion of Roman deities among the dramatis personae (e.g. Ceres, Cupid), the transformations of form and gender (e.g. those of Fidelia and Protea), and preoccupation with a single area of experience (sexual love) all combine to locate the work in a genre that makes few concessions to naturalism, and invites reflection not upon individualized experience but upon a topos or theme. Characters are grouped in oppositional relationships pertinent to the central concern (e.g. foresters and nymphs, Cupid and Ceres, Protea and the Siren), and embody contrasting positions rather than exhibiting a variety of traits, while speeches are non-naturalistic and elegantly structured, echoing one another, as noted above, in an emphatically stylized process of repetition and syllabic or syntactic variation. The action of the play is similarly patterned, lending itself to comparison with dance (see p. 21 above), while the events of the drama are largely symbolic (cf. Erisichthon's felling of Ceres' tree) rather than the product of a psychological process.

The on-stage structures signalling the locations in which the action takes place similarly stand, as in all Lyly's plays but for *Mother Bombie* and *The Woman in the Moon*, in a conceptual relationship with one another,[102] and are devoid of historical or culture-specific connotations.[103] A 'symbolic presentational'[104] platform, rather than the arena for an imaginative recreation of a particular place, the playing space contributes to the exploration of the polarities set up in the course of the work through the antithetical arrangement of 'houses' and the progress of characters between areas of the stage. Directions embedded in the dialogue (cf. 'I will hang my scutcheon on this tree in honour of Ceres': 1.1.32–3; 'This is the temple of our great god': 4.1.1; 'Ay me, behold, a Siren haunts this shore': 4.2.25) establish the division of the playing space into three discrete locations, representative of contrasting stances towards sexual desire: Ceres' grove (represented by her sacred tree), emblematic of unqualified adherence to the virgin state; Cupid's temple, symbolic of chaste (i.e. faithful) love; and a sea-shore dominated by the rock of a Siren, denoting unselective, destructive lust. Entry to and movement between these locations is carefully choreographed. Act 2, for example, opens before Ceres' tree, signalled by the comment that 'Here lieth the tree, hacked in pieces' (2.1.5–6), but a movement across the stage towards the temple of Cupid is then indicated by the series of injunctions and announcements which punctuate the ensuing exchange (cf. 'But let us to the temple of Cupid': 2.1.45; 'Well, let us to Cupid': 2.1.85; 'This is the temple': 2.1.93). The progress from one location to the other enacts the introduction of the nymphs to a new area of experience, and a similar process is implied in Protea's metatheatrical injunction to Petulius, following the latter's encounter with the Siren, to 'Follow me at this door, and out at the other' (4.2.112), enabling her own transformation and denoting his removal from unselective lust to love.[105] The directions indicate that staging, as in the majority of Lyly's plays, was simultaneous, with the three 'houses' present on the stage at the same time,[106] but the play differs from a number of items in the corpus in that while the significance of the different areas of the playing space remain constant, some changes of set take place.[107] Ceres' tree, emblematic at the outset of the unyielding virginal condition, is replaced between Acts 4 and 5 by the rock, the flower, and the bird into which Nisa, Celia, and Niobe have been transformed for their resistance to love, while the three objects themselves disappear in the course of the final scene (possibly by means of some species of *periaktos*)[108] when the nymphs regain their human shape.[109]

While the use of simultaneous, antithetical staging is characteristic of Lyly's work, its deployment in *Love's Metamorphosis* is unusual in the close proximity that the dramatist establishes between character and location. Whereas Diogenes' tub in *Campaspe* functions solely as an index of the austerity of his life, and Sappho's bed in *Sappho and Phao* is a free-standing structure denoting the Queen's preoccupation with amatory affairs, Ceres' tree occupies a liminal position between a setting and a part, in that, while functioning as a site, emblematic of devotion to Ceres (cf. the ceremonies enacted in the opening scenes of the play), it/she is simultaneously an arborified nymph, capable of human emotions and speech (cf. 1.2.107ff.).[110] Similarly, the rock, flower, and bird that replace Ceres' tree in the latter stages of the play are at once objects symbolic of particular states of mind and Ceres' followers in their translated forms, while the Siren's rock and the Siren herself are inseparable, jointly expressive of the allure and danger of sexual love. The intellectual arena evoked through the on-stage structures of *Campaspe* and *Sappho and Phao* has thus given way in *Love's Metamorphosis* to a world much closer to that of Ovidian myth, in which human and non-human forms are interchangeable, and processes of mutation and elision are constantly at work. Rather than simply contributing to a species of debate by means of their arrangement, the locations thus combine with other elements of the drama to initiate the audience into an inherently unstable world, and are themselves productive of wonder through the transformations they undergo (see pp. 37–8 below).

Like the settings, the props required by the action function as extensions of the dramatis personae rather than as instruments to advance the progress of events. Whereas the portrait commissioned by Alexander in *Campaspe*, for example, allows the artist access to the woman he loves, and the letter, ring, and bloody napkin of *The Woman in the Moon* are the means by which the title figure exacts her revenge on the lovers who have betrayed her, the objects carried by the dramatis personae in *Love's Metamorphosis* are inseparable from the characters themselves, and contribute to the definition of the stances they embody. The garlands with which the nymphs do honour to Ceres in 1.2, for example, differentiate their personalities and define their stances towards sexual love; the white doves offered in 2.1 by Ceres to Cupid are an index of the purity of her mind; while the mirror and comb of the Siren in 4.2 denote her obsession with her own seductive allure. While functioning as emblems of states of being (cf. 'You see their posies is as their hearts': 3.1.183), the properties thus contribute to the easy interchange set up by the drama between the human and non-human spheres, destabilizing the boundary between disparate aspects of the natural world (cf. Celia's identification of herself with her garland in 'I am content to wither before I be worn': 1.2.14–15).

It is the much greater reliance upon spectacular effects, however, that most obviously differentiates *Love's Metamorphosis* from other items in the Lylian canon. Though the 'houses' denoting the disparate locations in which the action take place belong to a common stock of theatrical effects,[111] Lyly's use of them differs markedly from his practice in other plays. A tree, for example, plays a significant part in the action of *Galatea*, functioning initially as a means of shelter from the heat of the sun, and subsequently as the site of the virgin sacrifice which threatens the life of the title figure, while a twig, on stage in the early acts of *Endymion*, is later replaced by a full-grown tree (signalling the passage of time) which is then revealed to be the arborified Bagoa. In the first instance, though the significance of the property alters in the course of the action, the tree itself remains unchanged, while in the second, though some species of special effect is involved in Bagoa's return to human shape,[112] her arborified form is of minor importance in the scheme of the drama as a whole. In *Love's Metamorphosis* by contrast, the tree is central to the increasingly spectacular sequence of effects that reaches its climax at the close of Act 1. Initially the focal point of rituals in honour of Ceres, it is first decorated with scutcheons and garlands, and then honoured with song and dance, before being attacked with an axe by Erisichthon, unexpectedly bleeding and emitting groans, and uttering a lengthy speech before being felled and dismembered (cf. 2.1.5–6).[113] Similarly, the rock, which stands in an antithetical relationship to Ceres' tree, is the site of a number of equally striking theatrical effects. A Siren is disclosed on (or rises from) it in the course of 4.2, singing and combing her hair,[114] and appears to 'shrink' (4.2.109) back into it again at the close of the scene, while it is by passing through the adjacent door and re-emerging at a different point on the stage that Protea is transformed from an old man (Ulysses) into her own shape. It is in the closing scene of the drama, however, that the most spectacular of the play's events takes place. Having reached an agreement with Ceres, Cupid invokes the aid of Venus to restore the nymphs to human form, calling upon her to 'send down that shower wherewith thou wert wont to wash those that do thee worship', and to let 'love, by thy beams, be honoured in all the world, and feared, wished for, and wondered at' (5.4.39–42). The invocation clearly signals the descent of some species of shower from which the maidens emerge, while the three objects into which they had been transformed for their resistance to Cupid disappear simultaneously from view.[115] Stage properties are thus employed by the dramatist in this play not simply to signify mental and physical positions but to evoke wonder and surprise throughout, at once moving the audience to 'inward delight'[116] and enacting the transformatory character of love.

Though the 1601 quarto lacks the detailed directions that distinguish the text of *The Woman in the Moon*, the dialogue offers a number of indications that the physical appearance of the dramatis personae also contributed to the promotion of love as a state to be 'feared, wished for, and wondered at'. In Act 1, for example, the 'fair faces' (1.2.73) of Ceres' nymphs plainly contrast with the 'stern looks' and 'unkempt' locks (1.2.78 and 79) of Erisichthon, while in 4.2 the 'golden' hair (4.2.48) and 'bewitching beauty' (4.2.54) of the Siren's face conflicts with the remainder of her body, which is 'all fish, and feathers, and filth' (4.2.103–4).[117] The careful preparation for the entrance of Cupid suggests that his appearance was designed to be striking, and probably at odds with literary convention. Nisa derides the notion of a blind, naked, winged boy, with bow, arrows, and firebrands (2.1.59ff.), and Ceres' terse response to her comments, 'Well, Nisa, thou shalt see him' (2.1.73), implies that he will prove a formidable presence (cf. the authority with which he speaks throughout). Contemporary evidence of costuming for similar productions suggests, moreover, that textual indicators of beauty or ugliness were translated into dress. An inventory from 1560 in the Office of the Revels, for example, notes a group of elaborate costumes designed for Diana and her nymphs (cf. Ceres and her followers), including 'one vpper garmente and one nether garmente of purple Clothe of sylver', for the goddess herself, 'the vpper garment frenged with narrowe frenge of Cullen [Cologne] golde',[118] and comparably rich costumes for her attendants. With similarly elaborate attire for Erisichthon, Cupid, and the Siren, the costumes, in conjunction with the 'houses' and emblematic properties, would have afforded a series of enchanting visual effects, appropriate both to the genre of the play and to the courtly arena in which it was performed.

With its highly patterned, non-naturalistic action and reliance upon the promotion of meaning by non-verbal as well as verbal means, the play is perfectly crafted to exploit the talents of the young actors for whom it was designed. Though characters are clearly differentiated by the stances they assume,[119] their positions are stated rather than enacted, placing minimal strain on the actors' histrionic skills, and explored through oppositional relationships rather than the voicing of inner conflicts. The preponderance of female and juvenile roles is similarly undemanding in terms of representation, while the sequential process of 'numbering down the line' (see pp. 20–1 above) lends itself to enactment by a company trained to perform as a troupe. The musical abilities and youthful athleticism of the young players are exploited through song (cf. 1.2.67.1, 3.1.147.1, 4.2.51.1, and 4.2.56.1) and dance (cf. 1.2.67.1), while the subject matter is appropriate both to their years and academic education, in that it is concerned with the doubts and hesitations surrounding the transition from the virgin state to sexual maturity, and draws on a familiar classroom text. Provision is made, moreover, for the less able, or inexperienced, members of the troupe. The three-line part of Tirtena, for example, may have been designed as a trainee role (cf. the four-line part of Camilla in *Midas*, and the mute Ganymede of *The Woman in the Moon*), though the role could have been doubled, if necessary, with that of the Siren who does not appear until 4.2. At the same time, however, the drama bears witness to the demands that Lyly was able to make of his young performers. The death of Fidelia, for example, requires the convincing execution of an uninterrupted forty-eight-line speech (cf. Hebe's lengthy lament prior to her expected sacrifice in *Galatea*), while the part of Protea involves not only a range of attitudes and tones (e.g. in exchanges with Erisichthon, the Merchant, and Petulius) but the ability to play both a strong-minded young woman and an old man (cf. Pandora's shifting personality in *The Woman in the Moon*).

Judged by Hunter to be 'one of the best of Lyly's plays',[120] and celebrated by Daniel as 'an exquisite example of a minor kind of drama',[121] *Love's Metamorphosis* has met with considerable critical approval. For Parnell it is remarkable for the 'subtlety and distinction'[122] of its thought, while for Houppert it is 'Lyly's most exciting comedy', and one 'likely to appeal to an audience vague about the details of Elizabethan social history'.[123] Its revival during the dramatist's lifetime may point to its contemporary success, but there is nevertheless no record of any production of the work after its performance at the close of the sixteenth century by the Children of the Chapel. Rarely edited (see below), and never performed on the post-Renaissance stage, it remains, in the words of Carter Daniel, 'one of the most unjustly neglected'[124] of Elizabethan plays.

THIS EDITION

Love's Metamorphosis appeared in only one early edition, the quarto of 1601 (see pp. 1–4 above), which thus forms the basis of the present work. Only three editions of the play have subsequently been published: an old-spelling edition by F. W. Fairholt (1858), the monumental old-spelling edition by R. W. Bond (Oxford, 1902), generally cited in contemporary criticism, and a lightly annotated modern-spelling edition by Carter A. Daniel (Lewisburg, 1988). The play has also been edited by Donald James Edge in his unpublished PhD dissertation, *Critical Editions of John Lyly's 'Endymion' and 'Love's Metamorphosis'* (University of Rochester, New York, 1973). All four have been collated for the present volume, and variant readings recorded in the notes. Direct indebtedness to the work of previous editors is acknowledged in the commentary, but it is impossible to record the innumerable instances in which their decisions informed the choices made here, or their observations opened up a fresh avenue of enquiry.

The play is edited in accordance with the practices set out in the General Editors' preface.

NOTES

1 Greg, i, p. 17.
2 Stafford had printed six plays (for Burby, Wise, Aspley, and Burre) in the course of the previous two years, and was thus experienced in the handling of play texts.

3 The final page of the Houghton copy bears the device used on the title page (McKerrow 331) in place of the woodcut that appears in the other surviving quartos (McKerrow 312). Dr Stoneman (Florence Fearrington Librarian of the Houghton Library) informs me, however, that the paper on which the device is printed is smoother than that used for the rest of the book, the chain links do not correspond with G1 across the gutter, and the wire lines also appear to be different from those of the penultimate leaf. In all, the evidence suggests that the page was appended to the book at some stage in its history, to make good a defective copy of the text (cf. the copy of *Old Fortunatus* in the Houghton collection), and thus that the aberrant device is not relevant to the printing of the quarto.

4 A further speech prefix is omitted on B1r (1.1.1) in accordance with the practice of omitting the first speech prefix when the speaker is the character named first in the massed entry.

5 In the British Library (162.i.53, C.34.d.11, C.34.d.12); the Victoria and Albert Museum (Dyce 26, Box 26/1); Bodleian Library (Mal. 251 (7)); Worcester College, Oxford (Plays 3.23 (3)); Magdalene College, Cambridge (Pepys Library, PL 1102(7)); Saint Paul's Cathedral Library (shelfmark withheld); Folger Shakespeare Library (STC 17082); Harry Ransom Humanities Research Center (University of Texas at Austin (Pforz., 632); Houghton Library, Harvard (STC 17082); Huntington Library (62386); and Lilly Library, University of Indiana, Bloomington (PR 2659.L9.L6). The majority of copies are defective, lacking A1 (folded back in the Folger copy and used to re-back G2), A2 in two instances (BL C.34.d.12 and St Paul's), and, in six instances, G2 (BL (3), Bodleian, Pepys, and the suspect Houghton Library copy).

6 See Bevington, in Bevington, ed., *Endymion*, p. 3, and Hunter and Bevington, eds, *Galatea: Midas*, p. 112.

7 Bevington, ed., *Endymion*, p. 7.

8 The quarto of *The Woman in the Moon* is unique among early editions of Lyly's plays in its precise detailing of stage business and costume.

9 Cf. Bevington, ed., *Endymion*, p. 3.

10 A large number of directions are, however, embedded in the text. In 1.2, for example, Nisa comments, 'but see, the tree powreth out bloud, and I heare a voice' (B3r / 1.2.102–3); in 2.1 Ceres offers Cupid 'these white and spotlesse Doues' (C1v / 2.1.100–1); while in 4.2 Protea tells Petulius to 'Followe me at this doore, and out at the other' (E3r / 4.2.112). For a full discussion of the staging of the play see pp. 34–9 below.

11 Cf. the declarative or imperative mode of a number of directions (e.g. '*Cantant*': C4v / 3.1.147.1; '*Sing*': E2r / 4.2.51.1), indicating that the writer was thinking in terms of theatrical practice.

12 The figures for *Sappho and Phao*, *Galatea*, and *Mother Bombie* derive from the Malone Society editions of the plays. I am indebted to Edge (p. 18) for the line count for *Love's Metamorphosis*.

13 For the possibility that the Protea / Petulius interest might have occupied the same position as the young servant plots of other plays see n. 40 below.

14 Edge, pp. 15–18. All quotations in the course of this paragraph are from pp. 17–18.

15 Compare 'Actus terius [*sic*], Schaena prima' for 'Actus tertius, Schaena quarta' (*Q1*, *Sappho and Phao*) and 'Act. 2. Sce. 2' for 'Act. 1. Sce. 2' (*Q1*, *Mother Bombie*). *Q2* of *Mother Bombie* has further errors.

16 The running-title on D2r of the Houghton Library copy of the play is followed by a subtitle beginning 'or lou[?]es a[?]' which has unfortunately been cropped. Too little of the note survives, however, to permit the dating of the hand, and there is no further evidence that the play was ever known by a different title.

17 The title-page of *The Woman in the Moon* states that the play is 'By IOHN LYLLIE maister / of Artes'. The other six comedies by Lyly published during the dramatist's lifetime are promoted as having been played by the Children of the Chapel and/or the Children of Paul's.

18 86v of Pudsey's manuscript begins with the heading: 'Love Metamorphosis Lilly & Alexander and Campaspe'.

19 The value of Pudsey's testimony is debatable in that he may have been working from the 1601 edition. His spelling of the name of the dramatist differs, however, from that on the title-page of the quarto, and the linking of the play with *Campaspe* implies some knowledge of Lyly's work.

20 A number of scholars have argued that *The Woman in the Moon* was designed for an adult troupe. For evidence that it was written for a boy company see pp. 3–9 of my edition of the play in the Revels series (2006).

21 Only two parts are for adult men (Erisichthon and the Merchant), while eight parts are for women (played by youths on the Renaissance stage), and five are for young men.

22 The theme is initiated in *Galatea*, 1.2, in which an unnamed nymph of Diana derides Cupid as a 'little god' (line 32), and is concluded in *Love's Metamorphosis*, after an emphatic display by the deity of his power, with Ceres' deferential reference to 'This great god' (5.4.48), and Cupid's assertion of the folly of making 'a mock of love, or a scorn of Cupid' (5.4.51–2).

23 For a more detailed account of the close relationship between *Galatea* and *Love's Metamorphosis* see Scragg, pp. 37–8.

24 Though Hebe is led to the place of sacrifice in *Galatea*, she is ultimately spared, while Fidelia in *Love's Metamorphosis* is slain.

25 There is a direct allusion to the action of the earlier play, for example, at 5.3.92–3.

26 For a full discussion of the dating of *Galatea*, see Hunter, in Hunter and Bevington, eds, *Galatea: Midas*, pp. 4–6.

27 Edge, for example, suggests 1584–85 as the 'probable date of composition' (p. 76); Saccio positions it as 'the last of Lyly's middle plays' (p. 161); while Hunter assigns it to 'the latter end of [Lyly's] career' (p. 81). Bond, opts for 1586–88 as the date of first performance (iii, p. 298), but concedes that it may have been written as late as 1599 (ii, p. 259).

28 Elements of three names, for example, are common to the two plays (see pp. 52–4nn. 6, 7, and 16), and the same Latin word is used in both

as an exclamation denoting 'of course' (cf. *Love's Metamorphosis*, 3.1.182 and *Midas*, 1.2.40). Other parallels are recorded in the notes.

29 Bond, iii, p. 293.

30 Hunter notes, for example, that '*Love's Metamorphosis* draws on Greene's *Alcida* . . . and so must be later than it' (p. 81).

31 As Bond himself notes, there is no allegorical representation of Famine in *The Faerie Queene* (iii, p. 293). The resemblances between Lyly's emaciated figure and Spenser's Despair, Doubt, etc. is thus generic rather than specific.

32 Edge, pp. 63–71. Among the principal points made by Edge are: that parallelism is not conclusive evidence of indebtedness, since 'authors copy themselves, copy each other, copy others, and there is no clear indication of how or where it all begins'; that the single passage shared by the two texts is 'remarkably ordinary' and 'sounds like simple proverb lore'; that Lyly's plot is closer to a tale by Boccaccio than to the plot of Greene's romance; and that the tenor of Greene's story links it with the latter phase of the writer's career, while the echoes of *Galatea* associate *Love's Metamorphosis* with Lyly's early work. For the contrary view that Lyly is indebted to Greene see Friedrich Brie, 'Lyly und Greene', *Englische Studien* XLII (1910), 217–22, and Rene Pruvost, *Robert Greene et ses Romans* (Paris, 1938).

33 The likelihood that Greene is indebted to Lyly rather than Lyly to Greene is supported by the fact that Greene's readiness to draw on Lyly's work is well attested (compare his exploitation of the vogue created by the publication of the two parts of *Euphues* with his *Euphues, his Censure of Philautus*), whereas Lyly rarely uses Greene's work. Edge notes that 'Greene was the staunchest of young Euphuists, and almost all his work up to *Menaphon* (1589) is filled with the matter and manner of Lyly's courtly fiction' (p. 70).

34 The natures of the three daughters of Alcida, around which the story is structured, look back, for example, to the dispositions of the daughters of a merchant in a tale related in *Euphues and His England*.

35 *Campaspe*, *Sappho and Phao*, *Galatea*, *Endymion*, and *Midas*.

36 The references to *Galatea* in the course of the drama imply that the two plays were written for the same audience, and were sufficiently close in date to permit the spectators to remember the plot of the earlier play.

37 It is possible, however, that the use of the term 'courtly' may merely indicate a general awareness on the part of the publisher that the play had been performed at court, but that details of the occasion were not available to him (see Saccio, p. 11n.).

38 Bond, iii, p. 297.

39 He claims, for example, that 'in Erisichthon, so ungrateful for the bounty Ceres has showered upon him, we have an allusion to Essex . . . and his presumptuous attitude towards the Queen in 1598, 1599, and 1600' (iii, p. 297).

40 The isolated example of overt satire on contemporary social conditions in 3.2 may lend some weight, however, to Bond's position. It is possible that Protea's sale to the Merchant may have been designed as the first of a trio of transactions satirizing the estates of the realm (the Merchant, the Soldier, and the Divine), and that the last may have proved overly

contentious. Some support for the argument may be gleaned from the trio of satirical encounters in the sub-plot of the related play, *Galatea*.

41 See Hunter, for example, p. 289.

42 Edge, for example, associates the play with Percy's *Arabia Sitiens*, *The Cuck-Queanes and Cuckolds Errants*, and *The Faery Pastorall* (pp. 18–19). Number of lines may not correlate, however, with playing time, given the play's heavy reliance on visual and aural effects (see pp. 37–9 below).

43 Compare *Love's Metamorphosis*, 4.1.44ff. and 5.4.55ff. with *AYL*, 5.2.81ff. For verbal echoes see notes to 1.2.39–40 and 1.2.45–6.

44 Quoted from *Ben Jonson*, ed. C. H. Herford and Percy Simpson, iv (Oxford, 1932). An earlier comment in the Induction on the significance of the fact that the play concerns Cupid ('that's a thing to be noted, take anie of our play-bookes without a CVPID, or a MERCVRY in it, and burne it for an heretique in *Poetrie*') also points to the probability that he had Lyly's play in mind, while suggesting that the older writer was still dictating fashion, in some respects, rather than falling behind it (lines 46–9).

45 See Hunter, pp. 289–90.

46 I am indebted for the following account of the history of the Erisichthon story to Hollis, pp. 128–32.

47 Hollis notes that at the close of the nineteenth century Jacob Zarraftis heard a tale called 'Mymmidonia and Pharaonia' on the island of Cos, in the course of which a prince orders his servants to cut down an oak, concealing a maiden, Dimitroula, who bleeds and curses him as she dies. He is attacked by hunger as a punishment, resorts to the sale of his children in order to feed himself, and finally consumes his own body. As Hollis notes, however, the story may not be a direct survival from antiquity but may itself be a product of the literary tradition (pp. 130–1).

48 A number of maidens in Ovid's poem are transformed, like Lyly's Nisa and Celia, into inanimate objects, while others, like Lyly's Niobe, become birds. Anaxarete, guilty of 'stonny hardnesse', is turned to marble (bk xiv, 872) while the Pierides of bk v become magpies.

49 A rather closer correspondence has been noted by Violet M. Jeffery between the strand of the plot turning on the metamorphosis of the three nymphs and an episode in Boccaccio's *Filocolo* (*John Lyly and the Italian Renaissance*, Paris, 1928, pp. 87–91). As Edge points out, however, Boccaccio's work was not translated into English and there are no verbal echoes to link the two compositions. Nevertheless, the fact that the defects of Ceres' followers coincide with those of Boccaccio's transformed maidens may indicate that Lyly drew on some Latin or English version of the story that has not yet been traced. For a full discussion of Jeffery's argument see Edge, pp. 122–5.

50 For a detailed discussion of the range of courtly entertainments informing Lyly's work see Hunter, pp. 114–58.

51 E.g. lyric (cf. Spenser's *The Shepheardes Calender*), narrative (cf. Sidney's *Arcadia*), and dramatic (cf. Shakespeare's *As You Like It*).

52 Quoted from Bond, i, p. 425. A number of entertainments attributed to Lyly are included by Bond in vol. i. of his collected edition of Lyly's

works, including those at Theobalds, Cowdray, Elvetham, Quarrendon, Harefield, Bisham, and Sudeley. Among these, the last is of particular relevance to this discussion in that it involves the appearance of Daphne from a tree.

53 For a useful summary of the pastoral elements of Lyly's plays, see Lancashire, pp. 22–6. Lancashire claims that '37.5 per cent of [Lyly's] known plays [are] fully pastoral and another 25 per cent partially so' (p. 22). I am indebted to her discussion for a number of the examples of courtly entertainments cited above.

54 *The Honorable Entertainement gieuen to the Queenes Maiestie in Progresse, at Eluetham in Hampshire, by the right Honorable the Earle of Hertford* (1591), quoted from Bond, i, p. 439.

55 Compare the use of printers' devices on the title-pages of early printed books, the numerous collections of emblems published during the period (e.g. those by Wither (1635) and Quarles (1635)), and the highly symbolic pageants celebrating such public occasions as the inauguration of the Lord Mayor and the entry of the monarch into the City of London.

56 The universality achieved through the use of a shared visual language may be measured by the survival of many of the motifs deployed in the course of the drama into the pictorial vocabulary of the modern era. The turtle-dove presented by Ceres to Cupid requires no explanation for a twenty-first-century audience, and the same is true of the bleeding heart, pierced with an arrow, presented by Ramis to the god of love (4.1.9–10).

57 Though the myths in question do not originate with Ovid, they are all retold by him in the *Metamorphoses*, and would have been familiar through him to a sixteenth-century audience.

58 Compare *The Woman in the Moon*, which draws on Horace, Cicero, and Martial in addition to a range of Ovid's works.

59 Compare *Galatea* in which an action involving classical deities is set on the banks of the river Humber, and *The Woman in the Moon* in which Nature's earliest creations exhibit a knowledge of classical, medieval, and sixteenth-century culture.

60 Daniel, p. 314.

61 For a detailed discussion of the principal features of euphuistic prose, and their role in the projection of meaning in Lyly's work, see Barish, *passim*.

62 The term is deployed by Barish to denote the pervasive ambiguity promoted by Lyly through his use of the euphuistic mode.

63 The use of stichomythia is not exclusive to this passage. For other examples see 2.1.120–33 and 3.1.119–24.

64 For a fuller discussion of the argument outlined here, and the relationship between the euphuistic mode and Lylian dramaturgy as a whole see my 'Speaking Pictures: Style and Spectacle in Lylian Comedy', *English Studies* 86 (2005), 298–311.

65 Though the account offered here largely centres upon patterns of opposition turning upon the nature of love, other kinds of antithetical relationships are also set up. The opening speeches of the foresters, for example, are blasphemous, in that they express doubts regarding the

supremacy of love (Cupid), paralleling Erischthon's sacrilegious assault upon chastity (Ceres), while Fidelia is ready to accuse both Ceres and Cupid of actions contrary to the virtues they embody.

66 The term is drawn from Hunter, p. 344.

67 Niobe's metatheatrical observation that she 'yielded first in mind, though it be my course last to speak' (5.4.163–4) is indicative of the self-conscious artifice at work in the serial organization of the lovers' exchanges.

68 The sequential structuring of the scene looks back to the serial admissions of love by the nymphs of Diana in *Galatea*, 3.1, which also influenced 4.3 of Shakespeare's *Love's Labour's Lost* (see Scragg, pp. 41ff.).

69 I am indebted for this analogy to Hunter, who notes the 'dance-like progression' characteristic of Lylian comedy as a whole (p. 160)

70 The punning on 'base', 'double', and 'treble' forges a further link with *Galatea*, in which three would-be apprentices quibble on their ability to perform three-part songs (cf. 5.3.201–6).

71 The phrase is drawn from the Epilogue to *Sappho and Phao* (line 3), in which Lyly likens the experience of encountering that work to entering a maze.

72 For the contrary view that the play is remarkable for the exhaustiveness of its analysis see Scragg, pp. 38–40.

73 The phrase derives from an exchange between Manes and Psyllus in 3.2 of *Campaspe* illustrating the slipperiness of language.

74 Compare the debate between Euphues and Eubulus over the relationship between nature and nurture at the outset of *Anatomy* (pp. 35–42), and the gathering uncertainty that comes to surround the terms in which Alexander is praised in the opening scene of *Campaspe*.

75 For a detailed discussion of the relationships set up in the course of the play between sexual desire and the sustenance of the body see Dooley, *passim*, to which I am indebted at this point.

76 Hunter, for example, describes the work as 'one of the best of Lyly's plays' (p. 206), in that 'the clarity with which he has fixed the position of each character allows him to develop his anatomy of love with a constructive precision and economy we do not find elsewhere' (p. 207).

77 Bond, iii, p. 294.

78 Saccio, p. 164.

79 Dooley, para. 19.

80 Edge, pp. 294–5.

81 Daniel, p. 315.

82 Pincombe, p. 150.

83 Lancashire, pp. 34–5.

84 Houppert, p. 113.

85 Parnell, p. 2.

86 As noted above, *Love's Metamorphosis* is considerably shorter than the majority of Lyly's plays, and the absence of any species of framing device may supply further evidence of the loss (or excision) of material at some point in its transmission history.

87 For a detailed exploration of the sixteenth-century cult of the Virgin Queen see Philippa Berry, *Of Chastity and Power: Elizabethan Literature and the Unmarried Queen* (1989).

88 Bond, ii, p. 259. Bond's argument here depends upon the assumption that the play was revised late in 1599.

89 Hunter, pp. 212 and 211.

90 The outcome could be seen as a natural development from the conclusion of *Galatea*, however, in which the lovers declare their feelings to be chaste (5.3.145–9), while the play closes with an Epilogue exhorting the female spectators to yield to love.

91 *England*, p. 339.

92 The 'error' may, of course, be a diplomatic one.

93 The outright hostility detected by some commentators towards the proponents of virginity in the play may suggest, however, that the play may be read not in terms of advice but criticism of a court dedicated to an essentially sterile condition. See Dooley, *passim*.

94 Both this passage and Celia's later questioning of the necessity for women to yield to male desires (see below) are among those quoted in Pudsey's notebook (see above, p. 4), testifying to their interest for a contemporary spectator.

95 The concluding remarks of the nymphs to their lovers are also worthy of note in that they attribute any defects of character they may subsequently exhibit to the conditions imposed upon them by their suitors, implying that the vices conventionally attributed to women are not innate but the product of experience (cf. the construction of the character of Pandora in *The Woman in the Moon* through the malign influence of authority figures). Nisa attributes her future coldness to having been transformed into a rock (5.4.144–7), Celia explains her potential sharpness as the product of her period as a rose (5.4.153–7), while Niobe ascribes her latent inconstancy to her former life as a bird (5.4.164–6).

96 Pincombe asserts that 'there is no-one like her in the drama before Lyly' (p. 156).

97 See Pincombe, pp. 155–6. I am indebted to Pincombe's discussion of the figure of Protea for this point.

98 Houppert describes her as 'lovely, although slightly used' (p. 112), but there is no suggestion by the inhabitants of the play world that she is seen as tarnished by her relationship with Neptune.

99 Pincombe, p. 156.

100 The quotation is taken from the Epilogue to *Sappho and Phao*. The play (i.e. *Sappho and Phao*) is also likened in the same Epilogue to a 'maze', leaving the audience 'intangled' in 'doubts'.

101 *Mother Bombie* stands aside, in some respects, from the remainder of the corpus, in that, though the structure looks back to Roman New Comedy and the majority of the dramatis personae have classical names, the play is set in an English town (Rochester), and involves recognizable sixteenth-century characters and locations (e.g. a hackneyman, a scrivener, and an inn).

102 In *Campaspe*, for example, Diogenes' tub and Apelles' workshop embody contrasting attitudes to life (repression and celebration of the

senses), while in *Sappho and Phao* the cave of the aged Sybilla stands in opposition to the bedchamber of the youthful queen Sappho.

103 Though Cupid's temple appears to be an exception in that it is drawn from Graeco-Roman religious observances, the 'house' is evocative not of a particular period but of an attitude to the amatory state.

104 The term is drawn from Bevington in Hunter and Bevington, eds, *Campaspe: Sappho and Phao*, p. 184. Bevington's discussion (pp. 181ff.) provides a detailed account of both the resources available to the dramatist and the traditions on which he draws.

105 Bond supplies a stage direction indicating that the characters '*pass through the central structure*' (IV.ii.96.1), but it seems more probable that Protea's lines indicate that they exit through a door adjacent to the sea-shore ('this door'), and re-enter through Cupid's temple ('the other'), finally leaving the stage (see below) through Ceres' grove.

106 Ceres' tree presumably stood on one side of the stage and the rock of the Siren, its polar opposite, on the other, with Cupid's temple between them. See Saccio, p. 163.

107 *Endymion*, which may well be close in date to *Love's Metamorphosis*, also involves a number of changes of scene, some of which, as Bevington argues, may have been effected by the use of a painted curtain (see Bevington, ed., *Endymion*, pp. 50–6).

108 A three-sided device that could be revolved to display different scenes. See Hunter, in Hunter and Bevington, eds, *Campaspe: Sappho and Phao* (Introduction to *Campaspe*, n. 45), for a detailed discussion of the possibility that *periaktoi* were available to the dramatist at the first Blackfriars, for which the two plays related to *Love's Metamorphosis* were composed.

109 Support for the argument that the transformed nymphs are situated on the site formerly occupied by Ceres' tree is supplied by the conversation between Petulius and Protea at the close of Act 4, and an exchange between Cupid and Ceres at the start of Act 5. Having removed Petulius from the arena of the Siren (presumably to Cupid's temple), Protea draws her lover towards the site of the grove (cf. 'let us into the woods': 4.2.116), and it is on their re-entrance, presumably from the same side of the stage, that they encounter the nymphs in their transformed shapes (cf. 5.2.26ff.). The replacement of the tree, felled in Act 1 and still on-stage at the start of Act 2, is further supported by Cupid's comment that 'Diana hath changed [Fidelia's] blood to fresh flowers, which are to be seen on the ground' (5.1.41–2).

110 Though the arborified Bagoa in *Endymion* is superficially similar, the tree into which she is transformed does not constitute a significant site in the course of the play, and plays no part in the action prior to Bagoa's return to human form.

111 Sixteenth-century documents from the Office of the Revels, for example, record a 'Rocke, or hill ffor the ix musses to Singe vppone' (cf. Lyly's Siren) in an inventory of 1564, and expenditures over a number of years for 'Lodes of Tymber for the Rock', 'Canvas to paynte . . . greate hollow trees' (cf. Ceres' sacred tree), and 'Armes of Okes for the hollo tree' (Feuillerat, pp. 117, 244, 197, and 200).

112 Bevington suggests that the discovery of Bagoa may have been effected
    by the use of a curtain, 'since the lunary bank and its tree appear to
    have been located in a curtained space' (Bevington, ed., *Endymion*,
    p. 56).

113 There is no evidence of the means by which the last of these spectacles
    was effected, but an actor was probably concealed inside the trunk
    (cf. the 'hollo tree' listed in the Revels' inventory quoted above: n. 111),
    while the tree may have been assisted to the ground, in a flurry of
    concern, by the shocked nymphs. Logs could then have been substi-
    tuted for the fallen tree between the acts, allowing for the declaration
    that it had been 'hacked in pieces' (2.1.5–6).

114 Again, the staging mechanism deployed here is uncertain, but the rock,
    denoting the sea-shore, may have been on stage throughout, with the
    actor concealed within it, and emerging from it, in 4.2 (cf. the large
    three-dimensional rock constructed by the Revels Office for *The Knight
    of the Burning Rock* in 1579, from which the actor rose through a trap
    by means of an elevating chair (see Astington, p. 102)). Other possibili-
    ties include the use of a discovery space, concealed by a curtain depict-
    ing a sea-shore.

115 The text gives no indication how the spectacle was managed, but some
    species of *periaktos* may have been employed (see n. 108 above). Alter-
    natively, the nymphs may have emerged through a painted curtain, on
    which the shower was depicted, and which then concealed their inani-
    mate equivalents from view.

116 *Sappho and Phao*, Prologue at the Blackfriars, line 8.

117 It is not clear from the text, however, whether the nether portion of the
    Siren was visible to the audience (i.e. the contrast here may be verbal
    rather than visual).

118 Feuillerat, p. 43.

119 Differences are distinguishable within, as well as between, groups. The
    three nymphs display different facets of the Petrarchan mistress, while
    Ramis is the most absolute of the three foresters, ready to achieve his
    mistress at any price (cf. 'Let them curse all day, so I may have but one
    kiss at night': 5.3.21–2), Montanus the most eager to seek revenge (cf.
    3.1.188ff.), and Silvestris the most sensitive (cf. his suggestion that they
    visit the starving Erisichthon at 4.1.142, and uncertainty at 5.3.6–7 how
    to greet the nymphs whose transformation they have occasioned).

120 Hunter, p. 206.

121 Daniel, p. 315.

122 Parnell, p. 16.

123 Houppert, pp. 107 and 113.

124 Daniel, p. 314.

LOVE'S

METAMORPHOSIS

A
Witty and Courtly
Pastoral

WRITTEN BY

Mr John Lyly

First played by the Children of Paul's, and now
by the Children of the Chapel.

LONDON
Printed for William Wood, dwelling at the West end of
Paul's, at the sign of Time.   1601.

[Characters in Order of Appearance

RAMIS, *a forester, in love with Nisa.*
MONTANUS, *a forester, in love with Celia.*
SILVESTRIS, *a forester, in love with Niobe.*

NISA,
NIOBE, } *nymphs of Ceres.*   5
CELIA,

ERISICHTHON, *a boorish farmer, and self-proclaimed ruler of the*
forest.

Characters . . . Appearance] *not in Q; list first supplied by Fairholt and followed*
with minor changes by Bond, who standardizes Q ERISICTHON *as* ERISICH-
THON. *Edge and Daniel arrange names in order of appearance but the latter lists*
NIOBE *and* CELIA *in reverse order. The ordering of names in this ed. follows*
Daniel.

1, 2, 3. *RAMIS, MONTANUS, SILVESTRIS*] all names derived from Latin
and appropriate both to foresters and the pastoral setting of the play. Ramis
derives from *ramus*, a branch (cf. Ramia, a follower of the virgin huntress
Diana in *Galatea*); Montanus signifies mountain dweller (cf. the shepherd
lover of Lodge's *Rosalynde*, 1590); while Silvestris denotes one at home in
the woods (cf. Silvius in *AYL*). For the significance of the names in relation
to the date of the play see p. 10 above.
    4. *NISA*] a female proper name used by Vergil (cf. *Eclogues*, 8, 18), but
probably suggested in this instance, as Edge notes (p. 629), by Ovid's use
of the term 'virgo Niseia' (i.e. daughter of Nisus) for the unnaturally hard-
hearted Scylla of *Met.*, bk viii (LCL 35). The figure is frequently conflated
with the daughter of Phorcas, also named Scylla, a beautiful woman hostile
to suitors, who is changed into a rock in *Met.*, bk xiv.
    5. *NIOBE*] daughter of Tantalus, transformed into a stone (a fate trans-
ferred by Lyly to Nisa) for her immoderate pride in her offspring. The name
derives, as Edge points out (p. 629), from the Gk for 'snowy' and may have
been associated by Lyly with inconstancy (cf. 'nothing more fair than snow,
yet nothing less firm': *England*, p. 236).
    6. *CELIA*] derived from Latin *caeles* (heavenly), and indicative of beauty.
Lyly uses the name in *Midas* for the beloved of Eristus, who, like the Celia
of the play, is hostile to love. The name is used by Shakespeare for Rosalind's
cousin in *AYL* (see p. 10 above).
    7. *ERISICHTHON*] tearer up of the earth (from Gk *eris* = discord / chthon
= earth). The son of Triopos, a Thessalian king, Erisichthon cut down a
grove sacred to Ceres and was punished by the goddess with a raging hunger
(cf. Ovid, *Met.*, bk viii, 923ff. / LCL 738ff.). The first element of the name,

FIDELIA, *an arborified nymph of Ceres.*
CERES, *goddess of the harvest.* 10
TIRTENA, *a nymph attendant upon Ceres.*
CUPID, *god of love, and supreme deity of the play.*
PROTEA, *daughter of Erisichthon, in love with Petulius.*
MERCHANT, *Protea's prospective owner.*
SIREN. 15

---

with its suggestion of discord, forges a link with Eristus, the unrequited lover of Celia in *Midas.*

9. *FIDELIA*] the faithful one (from Latin *fidelis*, capable of trust). The name reflects the character's unswerving devotion to Ceres, and may be derived from that of the heroine of *The Rare Triumphs of Love and Fortune* (Anon., 1582), who is subject to the conflicting wills of the gods. Lyly draws on the anonymous play in *The Woman in the Moon.*

10. *CERES*] As goddess responsible for the abundance of the natural world, Ceres is traditionally associated with fertility. Her role in the play as the upholder of chastity may derive, however, from Ovid's account of the yearly feast in her honour in which 'for the space of thryce three nyghts [women] counted it a sin / To have the use of any man, or once too touche his skin' (*Met.*, bk x, 497–8 / LCL 434–5).

11. *TIRTENA*] The role played by Tirtena corresponds with that of Ovid's unnamed 'fayrie of the hill' sent by Ceres to instruct Famine to afflict Erisichthon (*Met.*, bk viii, 976ff. / LCL 784ff.). Edge suggests that the name derives from Latin *terrena* (earthy), and is thus appropriate to a follower of Ceres.

12. *CUPID*] Usually figured in Renaissance literature as a wayward child (cf. *Sappho and Phao*), the Cupid of *Love's Metamorphosis* is a powerful deity, embodying love in its largest aspects. The unusual opposition between the play's principal deities, conventionally representative of fertility and love, may have been suggested by Ceres' anger at the rape of her daughter Proserpine, prompted by Cupid in *Met.*, bk v (lines 433ff. / LCL 341ff.).

13. *PROTEA*] one capable of change. The name derives from that of a sea god (Proteus) in the service of Neptune who could alter his form at will, and may have been suggested by the passage preceding Ovid's account of the punishment of Erisichthon, in which his unnamed daughter is compared to the god in her capacity to change shape (cf. *Met.*, bk viii, 913–24 / LCL 728–37).

14. *MERCHANT*] uncharacterized in Ovid, but here the vehicle for a satiric attack on the social mobility of the increasingly affluent sixteenth-century merchant class.

15. *SIREN*] explicitly linked in 4.2 with the sea nymphs of the *Odyssey* who had the power to lure mariners to destruction with their songs, but conflated here with the mermaid with her fish-like body, and use of mirror and comb. The reference to her 'feathers' at 4.2.104 may arise from the fact that the Sirens of classical myth had female faces and the bodies of birds.

PETULIUS, *in love with Protea.*

SCENE: *a forest sacred to Ceres, the nearby Temple of Cupid, and the adjacent coast.*]

SCENE] *This ed.; Arcadia | Fairholt;* a forest sacred to Ceres *Daniel.*

---

16. PETULIUS] probably derived from Latin *petulans* (wanton) and thus appropriate to a youth susceptible, for all his love of Protea, to the Siren's allure. The name forges a further link with *Midas*, in that it is close to that of one of a group of pages and is indicative there of pertness. Edge links the name with Latin *patulus* (spreading), a term used of branches, and suggests that Petulius, like the other lovers of the play, may have been a forester (p. 630).

Act I

[Actus primus, Scena prima]

[*Enter to a tree sacred to Ceres*] RAMIS, MONTANUS, [*and*] SILVESTRIS [*with garlands and scutcheons*].

[*Ramis.*] I cannot see, Montanus, why it is feigned by the poets that Love sat upon the chaos and created the world, since in the world there is so little love.

1.1.0. Actus . . . prima] *Fairholt (in accordance with headings of subsequent acts in Q); [I,i.] Edge; Act I SCENE I Daniel. Not in Q. Bond supplies <At Ceres' Tree.>.* 0.1–2. SD] *Stage directions derive from the Quarto, with editorial amplification signalled by square brackets. The following collation notes record substantive changes only, as when new stage directions or portions of stage directions have been added. The collation notes do not record routine amplifications, such as the supplying of an [Enter] where the entry is clearly implied in the Quarto by the listing of the characters' names, or an [and] in a series of names. Minor departures from directions supplied by previous editors, such as the ordering of names, are not recorded.* 0.1–2. SD. *to a tree sacred to Ceres . . . with garlands and scutcheons*] *This ed.* 1. SP] *Fairholt.*

1.1.0.2. with garlands and scutcheons] Though Ramis refers in the course of the scene only to his 'scutcheon' (line 33), the fact that the foresters' offerings include garlands is indicated in 3.1, when they return to the grove to 'see whether our garlands be there which we hanged on that tree' (lines 164–5). The offerings and verses hung on the tree by both the foresters and the nymphs in the following scene may have been suggested by Ovid's description of the sacred oak that Erisichthon fells: 'Uppon it round hung fillets [ribbons, ornamental head bands], crownes, and tables [writing tablets, notes] many one' (*Met.*, bk viii, 931 / LCL 743–5).

scutcheons] aphetic variation of 'escutcheon' (heraldic shield). The term refers here to personal devices expressive of the foresters' devotion (cf. the shields presented by her suitors to Thaisa in *Per.*, 2.2). Compare the garlands emblematic of their natures carried by the nymphs in the next scene.

1. SP] omitted in *Q* (in accordance with the convention whereby the speaker is not specified when he or she is the first named in the massed entry). Montanus' response at line 4 confirms that Ramis is the speaker.

1–9.] Bond suggests (iii, p. 563) that the lines may derive from the views attributed to Parmenides and Hesiod in Aristotle's *Metaphysics*, 1.4, but the concepts questioned by Ramis and Montanus are closer to those of six-teenth-century Christian neoplatonism; cf. 'God hath created and framed [the world] by love, no doubt but love is dispersed and shed throughout the

Montanus. Ramis, thou canst not see that which cannot with
    reason be imagined; for if the divine virtues of Love had   5
    dispersed themselves through the powers of the world so
    forcibly as to make them take, by his influence, the forms
    and qualities impressed within them, no doubt they could
    not choose but savour more of his divinity.
Silvestris. I do not think Love hath any spark of divinity in   10
    him, since the end of his being is earthly. In the blood is
    he begot by the frail fires of the eye, and quenched by
    the frailer shadows of thought. What reason have we,
    then, to soothe his humour with such zeal, and follow his
    fading delights with such passion?   15
Ramis. We have bodies, Silvestris, and human bodies; which
    in their own natures being much more wretched than
    beasts, do much more miserably than beasts pursue their
    own ruins. And since it will ask longer labour and study
    to subdue the powers of our blood to the rule of the soul   20

11–12. is he] *Q;* he is *Bond.*

---

whole world' (Pierre de la Primaudaye, *The French Academy*, quoted from
Edge, p. 631). The heretical stance they adopt towards love (embodied here
in the play's supreme deity, Cupid) anticipates Erisichthon's blasphemous
challenge to Ceres in the following scene. In line 1, feigned = related in
fiction (Onions). Compare *3H6*: 'all that poets feign of bliss and joy'
(1.2.31).

    10–15.] The position adopted by Silvestris invites reflection upon the
nature of love, a common sixteenth-century debate motif. His stance that
love is sensual (cf. 'the end of his being is earthly'), rather than spiritual (cf.
'I do not think Love hath any spark of divinity in him') accords with that of
Philautus in *England*, where it is emphatically repudiated by Euphues (pp.
293–5). The concept that love is instigated by sight 'begot by the frail fires
of the eye') is a Renaissance commonplace; cf. 'Love cometh in at the eye'
(*England*, p. 206). Fairholt (ii, p. 283) cites the song on the nature of 'fancy'
in *MerVen.*: 'It is engend'red in the eyes, / With gazing fed' (3.2.67–8). For
a discussion of the play's exploration of the relationship between the physical, spiritual, and social aspects of love see pp. 22–6 above.

    11. *blood*] the seat of the passions.

    12–13. *quenched by . . . thought*] extinguished by the yet more insubstan-
tial workings of the mind.

    14. *soothe his humour*] pander to his wishes.

    19–20. *ask longer . . . soul*] require more hard work and thought to oblige
our physical selves to follow the dictates of our spiritual beings.

than to satisfy them with the fruition of our loves, let us
be constant in the world's errors, and seek our own
torments.

Montanus. As good yield indeed submissively, and satisfy part
of our affections, as be stubborn without ability to resist,   25
and enjoy none of them. I am in worst plight, since I love
a nymph that mocks love.

Ramis. And I one that hates love.

Silvestris. I one that thinks herself above love.

Ramis. Let us not dispute whose mistress is most bad, since   30
they be all cruel; nor which of our fortunes be most
froward, since they be all desperate. I will hang my
scutcheon on this tree in honour of Ceres, and write this
verse on the tree in hope of my success: *Penelopen ipsam
perstes modo tempore vinces.* Penelope will yield at last: 35
continue and conquer.

[*He hangs his offerings on the tree.*]

36.1. SD]   *This ed.*

22. *be constant . . . errors*] conform to the misguided priorities of the universe we inhabit.

23. *torments*] amatory sufferings.

24–6. *As good . . . them*] The lines depend on the assumption that love is
irresistible whatever stance the foresters adopt. Montanus argues that it is
better to yield to the promptings of passion and achieve some part of their
desires than to attempt, vainly, to stand aloof from love and forfeit its pleasures altogether.

26–9. *I love . . . above love*] The attitudes ascribed to the three nymphs
(derision, hostility to amatory commitment, and disdain) conform to those
of the conventional Petrarchan mistress.

30. *mistress*] object of male adoration. The term derives from the courtly
love tradition and does not carry its current connotations of illicit sexual
partner.

32. *froward . . . desperate*] intractable . . . past hope.

34–5. *Penelopen . . . vinces*] Courted by numerous suitors during the
long absence of her husband Odysseus, Penelope remained faithful until his
return. The quotation, translated by Ramis, is from Ovid (*Ars am.*, i, 477),
and expresses the hope that drives unrequited lovers to continue their
pursuit. The Loeb edition reads *persta*.

36.1, 38.1, 42.1.] Though Ramis declares his intention to 'write this verse
on the tree' (lines 33–4), implying writing on, or carving into, the bark, the
lovers probably attach their mottoes to their garlands before making their
offerings (cf. 3.1.174–6, where the foresters discover the nymphs' responses
when looking for their garlands). Orlando in *AYL* similarly hangs up his
verses to Rosalind (cf. 'Hang there my verse') while declaring that 'these

Montanus. I this: *Fructus abest facies cum bona teste caret.* Fair
    faces lose their favours if they admit no lovers.

[*He hangs his offerings on the tree.*]

Ramis. [*To Silvestris*] But why studiest thou? What wilt thou
    write for thy lady to read?   40

Silvestris. That which necessity maketh me to endure; love,
    reverence; wisdom, wonder at: *Rivalem patienter habe.*

[*He hangs his offerings on the tree.*]

Montanus. Come, let us every one to our walks. It may be we
    shall meet them walking.   *Exeunt.*

Actus primus, Scena secunda

[*Enter to the same tree*] NISA, NIOBE, [*and*] CELIA
[*with garlands*].

Nisa. It is time to hang up our garlands. This is our harvest
    holiday; we must both sing and dance in the honour of

38.1. SD] *This ed.*   39. SD] *Edge.*   42.1. SD] *This ed.*

1.2.0. Actus . . . secunda] *Q*; SCENA SECVNDA. – <*The Same.*> / *Bond;*
[I,ii.] *Edge;* SCENE 2 *Daniel.* 0.1–2. SD] *This ed.; Nisa, Celia, Niobe,
Fidelia, Erisicthon. / Q;* NISA, CELIA, NIOBE, FIDELIA, ERISICTHON.
<*Enter* NISA, CELIA, NIOBE.> / *Bond;* [*Enter*] Nisa, Celia, Niobe. / *Edge;
Enter* NISA, NIOBE *and* CELIA. / *Daniel.*   2. holiday] *Q (holyday).*

---

trees shall be my books, / And in their barks my thoughts I'll character'
(3.2.1–6).

    37. Fructus . . . caret] The quotation, translated by Montanus, is from
Ovid (*Ars am.,* iii, 398). Lyly translates it more literally in *Sappho and Phao*
(cf. 'Fair faces have no fruits if they have no witnesses': 2.1.103–4).

    38. favours] charms (cf. *Ham.,* 4.5.186, 'She turns to favour and to pret-
tiness'), but with a possible pun on 'favour', a token given by a lady to her
lover.

    39. studiest thou?] are you lost in thought?

    42. Rivalem patienter habe] Endure a rival patiently (Ovid, *Ars am.,* ii,
539).

    43. let us . . . walks] let each of us go to that part of the forest for which
he is responsible (cf. *OED* walk, sb. II. 10, 'a division of a forest placed in
charge of a forester').

    1.2.1–2. harvest holiday] religious festival in honour of Ceres, goddess of
the harvest.

    2–3. we must . . . Ceres] Compare Ovid's description of the ceremonies
performed around Ceres' sacred oak: 'Full oft / The woodnymphes under

Ceres. Of what colours or flowers is thine made of,
   Niobe?

Niobe. Of salamints, which in the morning are white, red at   5
   noon, and in the evening purple; for in my affections shall
   there be no stayedness but in unstayedness. But what is
   yours of, Nisa?

Nisa. Of holly, because it is most holy, which lovely green
   neither the sun's beams, nor the wind's blasts, can alter   10
   or diminish. But Celia, what garland have you?

Celia. Mine all of cypress leaves, which are broadest and
   beautifullest, yet beareth the least fruit; for beauty maketh
   the brightest show, being the slightest substance, and I

---

10. wind's] *Fairholt;* winds *Q;* winds' *Edge.*

---

neath this tree did fetch theyr frisks [perform their lively dance movements]
aloft, / And oftentymes with hand in hand they daunced in a round / About
the Trunk' (*Met.*, bk viii, 932–5 / LCL 746–50).

   5. *salamints*] an unknown plant, identified by Bond (iii, pp. 563–4) with
polion, a herb described by Pliny (xxi, 21) as having leaves 'white to the eye
in the morning, bright red at midday and sea blue at sundown' (quoted from
Bevington, ed., *Sappho and Phao*, 2.1.100n.). A reference to Polion occurs
in *Sappho and Phao*, where it is linked to the fading of female beauty, cf.:
'Make not too much of fading beauty, which is fair in the cradle and foul in
the grave, resembling polion, whose leaves are white in the morning and
blue before night' (2.1.98–101). The reference occurs in the same speech as
the quotation from Ovid echoed at 1.1.37 above, suggesting that the passage
may have been running in Lyly's mind at this point. Edge contends, however,
that Lyly was 'almost certainly speaking of *Calamintum*' (p. 633), said to
destroy 'a mannes talent' (Banckes's *Herbal*, 1572), though, as he notes, the
plant has none of the properties Lyly ascribes to salamint. For a fuller discussion of the term see Edge, ' "Salamints" in John Lyly's *Love's Metamorphosis*',
N&Q, 21 (1974), 286.

   7. *no stayedness . . . unstayedness*] no constancy except in inconstancy. The
paradoxical concept that change is the only constant in both earthly life and
the universe as a whole is a recurring motif in the Lylian corpus (cf. the
assertion in *Galatea* that Fortune is 'constant in nothing but inconstancy':
1.1.22–3).

   9–11. *holly . . . diminish*] Like the offerings of the other two nymphs,
Nisa's garland is emblematic of her nature in that like the holly she is impervious to assault.

   10. *sun's . . . blasts*] Compare the opening lines of the Epilogue to *Endymion*: 'A man walking abroad, the wind and sun strove for sovereignty; the
one with his blast, the other with his beams'.

   12–13. *cypress leaves . . . fruit*] As Bond notes (iii, p. 564), the analogy
probably has its origins in Pliny, xvi, 60, where the cypress is described as
'*natu morosa, fructu supervacua*'. Lyly uses the same simile in *Anatomy* in

am content to wither before I be worn, and deprive   15
myself of that which so many desire.

Niobe. Come, let us make an end, lest Ceres come and find
us slack in performing that which we owe. [*They approach
the tree.*] But soft, some have been here this morning
before us.   20

Nisa. The amorous foresters, or none; for in the woods they
have eaten so much wake-robin that they cannot sleep
for love.

Celia. Alas, poor souls, how ill love sounds in their lips, who,
telling a long tale of hunting, think they have bewrayed 25
a sad passion of love!

Niobe. Give them leave to love, since we have liberty to
choose; for as great sport do I take in coursing their tame
hearts as they do pains in hunting their wild harts.

Celia. Niobe, your affection is but pinned to your tongue,   30
which when you list you can unloose. But let us read what

18–19. SD] *This ed.*   24. souls] *Q (soules); fools Daniel.*   31. unloose.]
Fairholt; vnloose? Q.

---

relation to the deceptive allure of physical beauty; cf. 'the cypress tree
beareth a fair leaf but no fruit' (p. 49).

15. *wither . . . worn*] Fresh flowers were frequently used as a means of
personal adornment in the sixteenth century, and were discarded when they
faded (cf. 'Gentlemen use books as gentlewomen handle their flowers, who
in the morning stick them in their heads and at night strew them at their
heels': *Anatomy*, p. 30). Celia asserts that she is happy to age and lose her
beauty without becoming another's adornment (i.e. being won by a man).

16. *that which so many desire*] sexual union.

18. *that which we owe*] the duties we should perform.

19. *soft*] stay, stop.

21. *or none*] if anyone.

22. *wake-robin*] *arum maculatum*, commonly known as cuckoo-pint or
lords-and-ladies (*OED* 1). Inability to sleep is noted by Ovid as one of the
symptoms of love (*Ars am.*, i, 735).

25–6. *bewrayed a sad passion*] unfolded a serious emotional expression.

27. *leave*] permission, freedom.

28. *coursing*] chasing (principally used of hunting small game with
greyhounds).

29. *as they . . . harts*] The comparison carries a double meaning: (*a*) as
they take trouble in pursuing their wild deer; (*b*) as they suffer in trying to
capture the untamed hearts of those they pursue.

30. *affection . . . tongue*] love is rooted solely in words (and thus is readily
recanted).

31. *list*] wish.

they have written. [*She reads out Ramis' verse.*] '*Penelopen
ipsam perstes modo tempore vinces.*' That is for you, Nisa,
whom nothing will move, yet hope makes him hover.
Nisa. A fond hobby, to hover over an eagle.   35
Niobe. But foresters think all birds to be buntings. What's the
next? [*She reads out Montanus' verse.*] '*Fructus abest facies
cum bona teste caret.*' Celia, the forester gives you good
counsel: take your pennyworth whiles the market
serves.   40
Celia. I hope it will be market day till my death's day.
Nisa. Let me read too. [*She reads out Silvestris' verse.*] '*Rivalem
patienter habe.*' He toucheth you, Niobe, on the quick;
yet you see how patient he is in your inconstancy.
Niobe. Inconstancy is a vice which I will not swap for all the   45
virtues. Though I throw one off with my whole hand, I

---

32. SD] *This ed.*   37. SD] *This ed.*   42. SD] *This ed.*   44. inconstancy]
Bond (inconstancie*)*; constancie *Q, Daniel* (constancy*)*.

---

34. *hover*] tarry, wait attentively at hand. The implied analogy with the
behaviour of a predatory bird is developed in the following line.

35. *fond*] foolish (with a pun on 'fond' = doting).

hobby] small falcon. The analogy implies that Nisa (here identified with
the eagle) is more powerful and ruthless than her would-be pursuer.

36. *foresters . . . buntings*] huntsmen believe all birds are easy game. A
family of small, finch-like, ground-feeding birds, buntings are at the opposite
pole from the eagle, the high-soaring predator with which Nisa identifies
herself (cf. Tilley, G376: 'A Goshawk beats not at a bunting').

39–40. *take your . . . serves*] sell while there is a demand (proverbial,
Tilley, M670). Compare Ganymede's advice to Phoebe in *AYL*: 'Sell when
you can, you are not for all markets' (3.5.60). For a discussion of the echoes
of *Love's Metamorphosis* in *AYL* see p. 10 above.

41. *it will . . . death's day*] my beauty will make me desirable all my life.

43. *toucheth . . . quick*] speaks aptly of you (literally, 'strikes at your most
sensitive spot').

44. *inconstancy*] *Q* 'constancy' (see collation note) is patently an error, in
that it is Niobe's inconstancy which calls for Montanus' patience.

45–6. *Inconstancy . . . virtues*] Compare Orlando's response in *AYL* to
Jacques's criticism of his surrender to love: ''Tis a fault I will not change for
your best virtue' (3.2.279–80).

46–7. *Though I . . . finger*] However forcibly I reject him, I can draw him
back with the minimum of effort. The analogy is probably derived, as Croll
and Clemons suggest (p. 280), from Latin proverbs opposing the strength
of the little finger to that of the whole hand or entire body of a man. Lyly
reverses the analogy in *England* in the context of simulated resistance to a

can pull him again with my little finger. Let us encourage
them and write something! If they censure it favourably,
we know them fools; if angerly, we will say they are
froward.   50

Nisa. I will begin. [*She writes a response to Ramis.*] *Cedit amor
rebus: res age, tutus eris.*

Celia. Indeed, better to tell stars than be idle, yet better idle
than ill employed. Mine this. [*She writes a response to
Montanus.*] *Sat mihi si facies sit bene nota mihi.*   55

Niobe. You care for nothing but a glass, that is, a flatterer.

Nisa. Then all men are glasses.

Celia. Some glasses are true.

Niobe. No men are. But this is mine. [*She writes a response to
Silvestris.*] *Victoria tecum stabit.*   60

Nisa. Thou givest hope.

Niobe. He is worthy of it that is patient.

51, 54–5, 59–60. SD] *This ed.*

courtship: 'I seemed strait-laced, as one neither accustomed to such suits
nor willing to entertain such a servant; yet so warily, as putting him from
me with my little finger I drew him to me with my whole hand' (p. 219).

48. *censure*] judge.

50. *froward*] ill-humoured, perverse.

51–2. Cedit . . . eris] Love yields to business: be busy, and you will be
safe (Ovid, *Rem. am.*, 144). Euphues offers the same advice to Philautus
when warning of the dangers of idleness: 'Love gives place to labour. Labour
and thou shalt never love' (*Anatomy*, p. 92).

53–4. *better to tell . . . employed*] it is preferable to be engaged on a seemingly pointless activity than to do nothing, though it is better to do nothing
than to be engaged in wrong-doing (*tell* = count). Lyly uses a variant of the
same proverbial expression (see Tilley, I7) in *Anatomy*: 'they found Mistress
Lucilla and Livia, accompanied with other gentlewomen, neither being idle
nor well employed, but playing at cards' (p. 61).

55. Sat mihi . . . mihi] It is enough for me if my beauty is well-known to
me. Bond suggests (iii, p. 564) that the line derives from Ovid, *Her.*, xvii,
38, though the parallel is not exact. The flirtatious Lucilla in *Anatomy*
similarly remarks to Euphues, 'not that my beauty is unknown to myself'
(p. 65).

56. *glass*] mirror.

58. *are true*] (*a*) provide an accurate reflection (i.e. are truthful); (*b*) are
faithful.

60. Victoria tecum stabit] The response ('Victory will be with you') com-
pletes the line from Ovid inscribed by Silvestris at 1.1.42.

Celia. Let us sing, and so attend on Ceres; for this day,
  although into her heart never entered any motion of love,
  yet usually to the temple of Cupid she offereth two white   65
  doves, as entreating his favour, and one eagle, as commanding his power. *Praecibusque minas regaliter addet.*
                                              Cantant & saltant.

[*Enter* ERISICHTHON.]

Erisichthon. What noise is this? What assembly? What idolatry? Is the modesty of virgins turned to wantonness, the
  honour of Ceres accounted immortal, and Erisichthon,   70
  ruler of this forest, esteemed of no force? Impudent
  giglots that you are to disturb my game, or dare do
  honour to any but Erisichthon! It is not your fair faces as
  smooth as jet, nor your enticing eyes though they drew

---

67. *Praecibusque*] *Q* (*Praecibusq*). 67.1. SD] *Q* (*subst.*); *They sing and
dance.* / *Daniel.* 67.2. SD] *Bond.* 72. giglots] *Q;* giglets *Daniel.*

63. *attend on*] go to wait upon.
64. *motion*] impulse.
65. *usually*] customarily.
66. *doves*] thought to pair for life, and thus usually emblematic of constancy. Ceres indicates at 2.1.100–103, however, that her offering denotes
her unsullied virginity and the freedom of her heart from amatory
concerns.
  eagle] As king of the birds, the eagle is conventionally associated with
majesty and the exercise of power.
66–7. *commanding his power*] calling on his protection.
67. Praecibusque . . . addet] 'And with entreatance mingled threates as
did become a King' (Ovid, *Met.*, bk ii, 498 / LCL 397). The Loeb translation
reads, more aptly, 'and to . . . prayers adds threats in royal style'.
67.1. Cantant & saltant] They sing and dance. The text of the song is
not in *Q* (see p. 2 above).
67.2.] Following the entrance of Erisichthon, the action relies heavily on
Ovid, *Met.*, bk viii, 925ff. / LCL 738ff. See Introduction, pp. 10ff.
68–9. *What idolatry?*] Erisichthon's challenge to the divinity of Ceres
parallels the foresters' stance towards Cupid in the opening scene.
70. *accounted immortal*] considered divine.
71. *esteemed of no force*] regarded as of no account.
72. *giglots*] wantons.
  game] sport.
74. *jet*] probably black marble, noted for its smoothness (cf. T. Robinson
c. 1620, 'The battelments of smoothest Iett were made': *OED* A sb. 2). It
is possible, however, that Lyly was thinking of the compacted form of black
lignite, capable of a high polish and of attracting light objects when rubbed

iron like adamants, nor your filed speeches were they as   75
forcible as Thessalides', that shall make me any way
flexible.

Niobe. Erisichthon, thy stern looks joined with thy stout
speeches, thy words as unkempt as thy locks, were able
to affright men of bold courage, and to make us silly girls   80
frantic that are full of fear. But know thou, Erisichthon,
that were thy hands so unstayed as thy tongue, and th'one
as ready to execute mischief as the other to threaten it,
it should neither move our hearts to ask pity or remove
our bodies from this place. We are the handmaids of   85
divine Ceres. To fair Ceres is this holy tree dedicated; to
Ceres, by whose favour thyself livest, that art worthy to
perish.

---

76. Thessalides'] *Fairholt; Thessalides / Q.*   79. unkempt] *Daniel;* vnkembd
Q.   82. th'one] *Q;* the one *Daniel.*   85. of] *Q; not in Bond.*

(*OED* A sb. 1). The comparison would thus look forward to the following
analogy, which turns upon physical allure.

75. *adamants*] magnets.
filed] polished.

75–6. *as forcible as Thessalides'*] A number of explanations have been proposed for this analogy. Assuming that the point of the comparison is not
oratory but 'wanton arts', Bond suggests (iii, p. 564) that *Q Thessalides* is a
mistake 'arising from setting up type from an ignorant oral reading of Lyly's
MS' and that the person intended by Lyly was Messalina (third wife of the
Emperor Claudius, noted for her licentiousness). Edge rightly points out,
however, that the emphasis of the passage is, in fact, upon oratory, and
glosses 'Thessalides'' as 'Thessalian women (Latin *Thessalis, Thessalidis*),
i.e., Thessalian witches, who had a reputation for working wonders, such as
pulling the moon down from the sky by incantations' (see also Pincombe,
p. 152). It is possible, though, that Lyly was thinking of the three daughters
of the river Peneios, collectively known as the Thessalides, who were begged
by Leto, pregnant with Apollo and Artemis, to persuade their father to give
her shelter.

78. *stout*] haughty (cf. *2H6,* 1.1.185: 'As stout and proud as he were lord
of all').

79. *unkempt*] rough, unruly (literally 'uncombed').
80. *silly*] simple.
82. *so unstayed*] as ungoverned.
83. *execute mischief*] perform an evil action.
87. *by whose . . . livest*] Like all living creatures, Erisichthon is dependent
upon the natural abundance that Ceres promotes.

Erisichthon. Are you addicted to Ceres, that in spite of Erisi-
    chthon you will use these sacrifices? No, immodest girls,   90
    you shall see that I have neither regard of your sex, which
    men should tender, nor of your beauty, which foolish love
    would dote on, nor of your goddess, which none but
    peevish girls reverence. I will destroy this tree in despite
    of all; and that you may see my hand execute what my   95
    heart intendeth, and that no mean may appease my
    malice, my last word shall be the beginning of the first
    blow.   [*He sets his axe to the tree.*]
Celia. Out, alas! What hath he done?
Niobe. Ourselves, I fear, must also minister matter to his   100
    fury.
Nisa. Let him alone. [*The tree bleeds and groans.*] But see, the
    tree poureth out blood, and I hear a voice.
Erisichthon. What voice? If in the tree there be anybody, speak
    quickly, lest the next blow hit the tale out of thy   105
    mouth.

---

98. SD] *This ed.; Smites the trunk with his axe. | Bond; Strikes the tree with
his ax. | Edge;* ERISICHTHON *strikes at the tree. | Daniel.* 102. SD] *This
ed.*

89. *addicted*] dedicated.
90. *use*] perform.
92. *tender*] treat with consideration.
94. *peevish*] foolish (cf. *Mother Bombie*: 'Parents in these daies are growen
pieuish, they rocke their children in their cradles till they sleepe, and crosse
them about their bridals till their hearts ake': I.iii.90–2).
96. *mean*] instrument, agent (cf. *A&C*: 'This blows my heart. / If swift
thought break it not, a swifter mean / Shall outstrike thought': 4.6.35–7).
99. *Out*] An exclamation of dismay or indignation.
100. *minister*] supply.
102–3. *But see . . . voice*] Compare Ovid: 'Assoone as that his cursed hand
had wounded once the tree, / The blood came spinning from the carf
[cut] . . . / Streight from amid the tree as then / There issued such a sound . . .'
(*Met.*, bk viii, 949–59 / LCL 761–70). For a discussion of the stage spectacle
engineered here see pp. 37–8.
105–6. *hit . . . mouth*] anticipate you with blows. The threat, the first of
the extracts noted by Pudsey (see p. 4 above), is a variant of the proverbial
expression 'To take the tale out of one's mouth' (Tilley, T50). Compare *H5*:
'It is not well done, mark you now, to take the tales out of my mouth ere it
is made an end and finished' (4.7.41–3).

Fidelia. [*From within the tree*] Monster of men, hate of the
heavens, and to the earth a burden, what hath chaste
Fidelia committed? It is thy spite, Cupid, that, having no
power to wound my unspotted mind, procurest means to   110
mangle my tender body and by violence to gash those
sides that enclose a heart dedicate to virtue. Or is it that
savage satyr, that feeding his sensual appetite upon lust,
seeketh now to quench it with blood, that, being without
hope to attain my love, he may with cruelty end my life?   115
Or doth Ceres, whose nymph I have been many years, in
recompense of my inviolable faith, reward me with
unspeakable torments? Divine Phoebus, that pursued
Daphne till she was turned to a bay tree, ceased then to
trouble her. Ay, the gods are pitiful. And Cinyras, that   120
with fury followed his daughter, Myrrha, till she was

---

107. SD] *Edge (subst.); from the trunk* / *Bond;* FIDELIA *speaks from within the
tree.* / *Daniel (following line 106 this ed.).*   113. satyr] *Q (*satire; *also* Satyre
at 140 this ed.).   120. Ay] *Q (*I*).* Cinyras] *Bond; Cineras* / *Q.*
121. Myrrha] *Edge;* Miretia *Q; Mirrha* / *Bond.*

107–54.] This speech has no counterpart in *Met.*, bk viii, in which the
arborified nymph merely reveals that she was once a follower of Ceres and
promises that her death will be revenged (lines 959–62 / LCL 771–3). For a
comparable lament by an innocent virgin in the face of violent death see
Hebe's lengthy speech prior to her expected sacrifice to the monster, Agar
(*Galatea*, 5.2.8–60), which touches on similar themes (e.g. the relationship
between gods and men, and the value of chastity).

    109. *committed*] done.

    It . . . Cupid] The assumption may be seen as a further example of the
failure of Ceres' followers to grasp the nature of Cupid (previously shown
in the attitudes of the three nymphs to love). David Bevington suggests,
however, in a private letter, that the first two words of the sentence may
have been transposed by the compositor, allowing the sentence to be read
as a question rather than an assertion (cf. the questions that follow).

    110. *procurest means*] finds a way.

    112. *dedicate*] dedicated.

    113. *savage satyr*] See lines 138–40 below.

    118–20. *Divine . . . trouble her*] Having fallen in love with Daphne,
Phoebus (i.e. Apollo) pursued her until, having prayed for divine intervention, she was transformed into a laurel bush. The story is related by Ovid
in *Met.*, bk i, 545–700 / LCL 452–567.

    120–2. *Cinyras . . . myrrh tree*] Son of Apollo and King of Cyprus, Cinyras
was seduced by his daughter Myrrha and became the father by her of Adonis,
while Myrrha was transformed for her sins into a myrtle tree (see Ovid, *Met.*,
bk x, 327ff. / LCL 300ff.). Lucilla, in *Anatomy*, cites Myrrha's love for her
father, together with other instances of unnatural passion, as evidence of the

changed to a myrrh tree, left then to prosecute her. Yea,
parents are natural. Phoebus lamented the loss of his
friend, Cinyras of his child; but both gods and men either
forget or neglect the change of Fidelia – nay, follow her   125
after her change, to make her more miserable. So that
there is nothing more hateful than to be chaste, whose
bodies are followed in the world with lust, and prosecuted in the graves with tyranny; whose minds, the freer
they are from vice, their bodies are in the more danger   130
of mischief. So that they are not safe when they live,
because of men's love; nor, being changed, because of
their hates; nor, being dead, because of their defaming.
What is that chastity which so few women study to keep,
and both gods and men seek to violate? If only a naked   135
name, why are we so superstitious of a hollow sound? If
a rare virtue, why are men so careless of an exceeding
rareness? Go, ladies, tell Ceres I am that Fidelia that so
long knit garlands in her honour, and, chased with a
satyr, by prayer to the gods became turned to a tree;   140
whose body now is grown over with a rough bark, and
whose golden locks are covered with green leaves, yet
whose mind nothing can alter, neither the fear of death,
nor the torments. If Ceres seek no revenge, then let

---

122. myrrh] *Q* (Mirre). 123. loss] *Q*; love *Daniel.* 125. forget] *Q*;
forgot *Fairholt, Bond.*

---

unaccountability of love (p. 75). As Bond notes (iii, p. 565), *Q* 'Miretia' is
probably a misreading of Lyly's ms. (compare the variant forms of 'Myrrh'
in editions of *England* (Bond, ii, p. 131, line 28n.).

122. *left . . . prosecute her*] ceased to pursue her after that.

123. *are natural*] adhere to the system of bonds and obligations running
throughout the divinely ordered world.

124. *friend*] beloved, sweetheart. Compare *Meas*: 'He hath got his friend
with child' (1.4.29).

125. *forget*] Fairholt's 'forgot', followed by Bond (see collation note),
appears to be an error, and is not supported by a note in either edition.

change] transformation.

128–9. *prosecuted*] See 122n. above.

134. *study*] are diligently concerned.

135. *naked*] bare (i.e. devoid of substance).

136. *superstitious of*] extravagantly devoted to.

137. *rare*] (*a*) uncommon; (*b*) excellent.

careless] unregardful.

139. *knit*] knotted. Compare *R&J*: 'I'll have this knot knit up' (4.2.24).

virginity be not only the scorn of savage people, but the   145
spoil. But, alas, I feel my last blood to come, and therefore must end my last breath. Farewell, ladies, whose
lives are subject to many mischiefs; for if you be fair, it
is hard to be chaste, if chaste, impossible to be safe. If
you be young, you will quickly bend; if bend, you are   150
suddenly broken. If you be foul, you shall seldom be
flattered; if you be not flattered, you will ever be sorrowful. Beauty is a firm fickleness, youth a feeble stayedness,
deformity a continual sadness.   [*She dies.*]

Niobe. Thou monster, canst thou hear this without grief?   155

Erisichthon. Yea, and double your griefs with my blows.
                                   [*He fells the tree.*]

Nisa. Ah, poor Fidelia, the express pattern of chastity, and
example of misfortune!

Celia. Ah, cruel Erisichthon, that not only defacest these holy
trees, but murderest also this chaste nymph!   160

Erisichthon. Nymph or goddess, it skilleth not, for there is
none that Erisichthon careth for but Erisichthon. Let
Ceres, the lady of your harvest, revenge when she will –
nay, when she dares! And tell her this: that I am
Erisichthon.   165

Niobe. Thou art none of the gods.

Erisichthon. No, a contemner of the gods.

Nisa. And hopest thou to escape revenge, being but a man?

---

154. SD] *Bond (subst.).*   156.1. SD] *This ed.; He proceeds to fell the tree to
the ground. / Bond;* ERISICHTHON *cuts down the tree. / Daniel.*   159. defacest]
Q; defaceth *Fairholt, Bond.*

---

146. *spoil*] prey. Compare *Luc*: 'Leaving his spoil perplex'd in greater
pain' (line 733).

153. *firm fickleness . . . feeble stayedness*] steadfast changeability . . . weak
firmness. The paradoxical states defined here are characteristic of the view
of beauty and human life projected throughout the Lylian corpus.

157. *express*] exact.

159–60. *holy trees*] The use of the plural here may look back to the
account of Erisichthon's onslaught on Ceres' grove in *Met.*, bk viii, in which
more than one tree is assailed with axes and ropes.

161. *skilleth not*] doesn't matter.

167. *contemner*] scorner.

Erisichthon. Yea, I care not for revenge, being a man, and
    Erisichthon.   [*Exit.*]   170
Nisa. [*To her companions*] Come, let us to Ceres and complain
    of this unacquainted and incredible villain. If there be
    power in her deity, in her mind pity, or virtue in virginity,
    this monster cannot escape.   *Exeunt.*

---

170. SD] *This ed.*   171. SD] *This ed.*

169. *care not for*] am unconcerned about.
being a man] Compare Tilley, 'Revenge is womanish' (R91).
172. *unacquainted*] strange, unprecedented. Compare the description of
a conspiracy involving witchcraft in *Endymion* as an 'unacquainted and most
unnatural practice' (5.4.47–8).

Act 2

Actus secundus, Scena prima

[*Enter to the felled tree*] CERES [*with a pair of white doves*],
TIRTENA, NIOBE, NISA, [*and* CELIA].

Ceres. Doth Erisichthon offer force to my nymphs, and to my
deity disgrace? Have I stuffed his barns with fruitful
grain, and doth he stretch his hand against me with
intolerable pride? So it is, Ceres: thine eyes may witness
what thy nymphs have told. Here lieth the tree, hacked   5
in pieces, and the blood scarce cold of the fairest virgin.

2.1.0. Actus . . . prima] *Q;* ACTUS SECUNDUS *Fairholt;* [II,i.] *Edge; Act 2*
SCENE I *Daniel. Bond supplies <At* CERES' *Tree, with transfer to* CUPID'S
temple, ll. 39–80.> (error for 38–80, lines 45–92 this ed.). 0.1. SD] *Bracketed*
material this ed. 0.1–2. SD. CERES / TIRTENA . . . CELIA.] *Edge (subst.);*
Ceres, Niobe, Nisa, Cupid, Tirtena. / *Q;* CERES, NIOBE, NISA, CUPID,
TIRTENA. <*Enter* CERES, NIOBE, NISA, *and* TIRTENA.> / *Bond; Enter* CERES,
TIRTENA, NIOBE, *and* NISA. / *Daniel.*

2.1.0.1. Enter . . . doves] The scene of the action is indicated at lines 5–6
below, where Ceres indicates the hacked tree that was Fidelia, and the blood
on the ground. For the doves carried by Ceres see 1.2.65–6 and 2.1.100–1.

0.2. *NIOBE . . . CELIA*] As Edge points out, Ovid describes the three
nymphs as dressed 'in mourning weede [garments]' when they approach
Ceres following the death of the arborified nymph (*Met.*, bk viii, 967 / LCL
778–9). Given the dramatist's fidelity to his source at this point (see notes
to lines 12–14 and 22–31 below), it is possible that the poem may afford an
indication of costuming here.

and *CELIA*] Celia does not appear in the massed entry at the head of the
scene in *Q*, nor does she speak in the following exchange. There is no textual
evidence to indicate, however, that the three nymphs do not appear together
as a troop, as they do throughout, and it is clearly important to the action
that Celia is present, like Niobe and Nisa, to receive the advice of Cupid. It
is possible that the parts of Celia and Tirtena may have been doubled at
some stage in the history of the play (see Edge, II.i.o.1n.), but the configura-
tion of characters suggests that Tirtena was either designed as a trainee role
(cf. Ganymede in *The Woman in the Moon*), or, less probably, was doubled
with the Siren (see Introduction, p. 39 above).

5–6. *Here lieth . . . virgin*] As noted above, the references to the tree, and
the blood on the ground, indicate that the scene opens in Ceres' grove,
though the action is subsequently transferred to the temple of Cupid.

If this be thy cruelty, Cupid, I will no more hallow
thy temple with sacred vows; if thy cankered nature,
Erisichthon, thou shalt find as great misery as thou
showest malice. I am resolved of thy punishment, and   10
as speedy shall be my revenge as thy rigour barbarous.
Tirtena, on yonder hill, where never grew grain nor
leaf, where nothing is but barrenness and coldness,
fear and paleness, lieth Famine. Go to her, and say
that Ceres commandeth her to gnaw on the bowels of   15
Erisichthon, that his hunger may be as unquenchable as
his fury.

Tirtena. I obey. But how should I know her from others?

Ceres. Thou canst not miss of her, if thou remember but her
name; and that canst thou not forget, for that coming   20
near to the place thou shalt find gnawing in thy stomach.
She lieth gaping, and swalloweth naught but air; her face

---

12. Tirtena] *Fairholt; Tirtenae* / *Q.*

7–8. *If this . . . vows*] Compare Fidelia's assumption that Cupid may have
been responsible for her death (1.2.109–112). The proposition is a further
instance of the failure to fully comprehend the nature of Love that pervades
the play world.

7. *hallow*] do reverence to.

8. *if*] if this be a product of.

cankered] malignant.

10. *am resolved of*] have decided upon.

11. *rigour*] cruelty.

12. *Tirtena*] See p. 53, line 11n.

12–14. *where never grew . . . Famine*] Compare: 'A Dreerie place, a
wretched soyle, a barreine plot: no grayne, / No frute, no tree, is growing
there: but there dooth ay remayne / Unweeldsome cold, with trembling feare,
and palenesse white as clowt, / And foodlesse famin' (Ovid, *Met.*, bk viii,
980–3 / LCL 789–91). The ensuing description of Famine, and Tirtena's
encounter with her, are heavily dependent upon the passage of bk viii that
follows (see lines 22–31n. below).

15. *bowels*] stomach.

19. *miss of*] fail to recognize.

20. *for that*] because.

22–31. *her face . . . body*] Compare: 'Her face pale colourd was. / Hir
heare was harsh and shirle [sheared?], her eyes were sunken in her head. /
Her lyppes were hore [grey with mould] with filth, her teeth were furd and
rusty read; / Her skinne was starched, and so sheere [transparent] a man
myght well espye / The verie bowels in her bulk how every one did lye. / . . . /
In stead of belly was a space where belly should have beene' (Ovid, *Met.*,
bk viii, 994–1000 / LCL 801–5).

pale, and so lean that as easily thou mayest through the
very skin behold the bone as in a glass thy shadow. Her
hair long, black, and shaggy; her eyes sunk so far into   25
her head that she looketh out of the nape of her neck.
Her lips white, and rough; her teeth hollow, and red with
rustiness. Her skin so thin that thou mayest as lively make
an anatomy of her body as she were cut up with surgeons.
Her maw like a dry bladder; her heart swollen big with   30
wind; and all her bowels like snakes working in her body.
This monster when thou shalt behold, tell her my mind,
and return with speed.

Tirtena. I go, fearing more the sight of Famine than the
force.   35

Ceres. Take thou these few ears of corn, but let not Famine
so much as smell to them. And let her go aloof from
thee.

[*Exit* TIRTENA, *with some ears of grain.*]
Now shall Erisichthon see that Ceres is a great goddess,
as full of power as himself of pride, and as pitiless as he   40
presumptuous. How think you, ladies, is not this revenge
apt for so great injury?

Niobe. Yes, madam. To let men see they that contend with
the gods do but confound themselves.

---

29. up] *Q; not in Daniel.* surgeons] *Q (*Chirurgiõs*).* 30. swollen] *Q*
(swolne*).* 38.1. SD] *This ed.; Exit* TIRTENA. / *Bond.* 43. men see they]
Punctuation as Fairholt; men see, they *Q;* men see: they *Edge.*

---

24. *in a glass thy shadow*] your reflection in a mirror.
25–6. *her eyes . . . neck*] The description is among the passages from the
play quoted in Pudsey's commonplace book (86v). For further extracts noted
in the course of the act see lines 50–4 and 124–7 nn. below.
26. *nape*] back.
28. *rustiness*] discoloration through disuse.
28–9. *as lively . . . surgeons*] describe her body anatomically as accurately
as if she had been dissected by surgeons.
30. *maw*] stomach.
31. *bowels . . . working*] intestines . . . writhing.
35. *force*] effect.
36. *few . . . corn*] small quantity of grain, designed to ward off the effects
of hunger without attracting the notice of Famine.
37. *smell to*] sniff.
go aloof] keep away.
44. *confound themselves*] bring about their own downfall.

Ceres. But let us to the temple of Cupid and offer sacrifice.   45
   [*They begin to move to a different part of the stage.*] They
   that think it strange for chastity to humble itself to
   Cupid know neither the power of love nor the nature of
   virginity, th'one having absolute authority to command,
   the other difficulty to resist. And where such continual   50
   war is between love and virtue, there must be some
   parleys and continual perils. Cupid was never conquered,
   and therefore must be flattered; virginity hath, and therefore must be humble.
Nisa. Into my heart, madam, there did never enter any motion   55
   of love.
Ceres. Those that often say they cannot love, or will not love,
   certainly they love. Didst thou never see Cupid?

---

46. SD] *This ed.*

---

46. SD] The fact that the characters move to a different part of the stage
here is implicit in the terms employed by Ceres at lines 45 and 93 (cf. 'let
us to the temple of Cupid' / 'This is the temple'). The repetition of 'let us
to . . .' at line 85 suggests that they pause in the course of their progress, but
there is no textual indication of the point at which they come to a halt. The
precision of the stage directions embedded in the exchange works against
Bond's contention that 'we have here one of the imaginary transfers of scene
common upon the early stage' (iii, p. 566).

46–50. *They that . . . resist*] Those who think it odd for chastity to be
deferential to love do not understand either the power of Cupid or the nature
of virginity, the former being in a position to command, the latter having
little ability to resist love's might. As Bond points out, the attitude of Ceres
towards Cupid is in marked contrast to the aggressive stance of Diana in
Galatea, in which 'the attitude of Ceres and her nymphs, respectively, is
exactly reversed' (iii, p. 565).

49–50. *th'one . . . the other*] love . . . virginity.

50–4. *where such . . . humble*] The passage is the most extensive of the
extracts from the play in Pudsey's commonplace book (86v) where it is
slightly misquoted (omission of 'such').

52. *parleys*] discussions during cessations of hostility.

53. *virginity hath*] virginity has been conquered. Though capable of construction as a general reflection on the tendency of chastity to yield to love,
the observation may look back to the fate of Diana's nymphs in *Galatea*, to
which Ceres alludes at lines 87–90 and 117–18.

55. *motion*] impulse.

57–8. *Those that . . . they love*] Compare Ovid, *Rem. am.*: 'He who says
o'ermuch "I love not" is in love' (line 648).

Nisa. No, but I have heard him described at the full, and, as
I imagined, foolishly. First, that he should be a god blind   60
and naked, with wings, with bow, with arrows, with firebrands; swimming sometimes in the sea, and playing
sometimes on the shore; with many other devices which
the painters, being the poets' apes, have taken as great
pains to shadow as they to lie. Can I think that gods, that   65
command all things, would go naked? What should he
do with wings that knows not where to fly, or what with
arrows that sees not how to aim? The heart is a narrow
mark to hit, and rather requireth Argus' eyes to take level
than a blind boy to shoot at random. If he were fire, the   70
sea would quench those coals, or the flame turn him into
cinders.

---

64. poets'] *Q* (Poets). 69. Argus'] *Q* (Argus).

59. *at the full*] in detail.

60–3. *that he . . . shore*] Nisa's description of conventional representations
of Cupid accords with the handling of the god in earlier items in the Lylian
canon (cf. Venus' comment on seeing the condition to which her son has
been reduced by Diana in *Galatea*: 'Alas, poor boy, thy wings clipped, thy
brands quenched, thy bow burnt, and thy arrows broke' (5.3.100–1)). The
Cupid of *Love's Metamorphosis* is a far more impressive figure, closer to the
Eros of Hesiod, who governs the councils of gods and men (cf. *Theogony*,
lines 116ff.), than to the mischievous child of Roman and early modern
art.

61–2. *firebrands*] flaming torches, traditionally carried by Cupid to ignite
the fires of love.

64–5. *painters . . . lie*] visual artists have taken as much care to represent
as poets have to invent them. The notion that painters were mere imitators
of the creative fictions of poets, and the neoplatonic view that poets were
liars (ultimately derived from Plato's *Republic*), were both commonplaces in
the early modern period. Compare *Tim.*: APEMANTUS How now Poet? /
POET How now Philosopher? / APEMANTUS Thou liest. / POET Art not one?
/ APEMENTUS Yes. / POET Then I lie not. / APEMANTUS Art not a poet? /
POET Yes. / APEMANTUS Then thou liest (1.1.217–25).

65–72. *Can I . . . cinders*] Bond suggests (iii, p. 566) that Nisa's critique
of representations of Cupid may derive from Watson's *Hecatompathia*, 19.

69. *Argus' eyes*] the hundred eyes of Argus. Set by Juno to guard Io,
because he was thought to be all-seeing, Argus was charmed to sleep by
Mercury on the command of Jove, enabling the god to gain access to his
beloved. After Argus' death, his eyes were transplanted by Juno to the tail
of her favourite bird, the peacock. The story is recounted by Ovid (*Met.*,
bk i, 701–903 / LCL 568–723).

level] aim.

Ceres. Well, Nisa, thou shalt see him.

Nisa. I fear Niobe hath felt him.

Niobe. Not I, madam. Yet must I confess that oftentimes I   75
have had sweet thoughts, sometimes hard conceits;
betwixt both, a kind of yielding. I know not what, but
certainly I think it is not love. Sigh, I can, and find ease
in melancholy; smile, I do, and take pleasure in imagination. I feel in myself a pleasing pain, a chill heat, a delicate   80
bitterness. How to term it, I know not. Without doubt it
may be love; sure I am it is not hate.

Nisa. Niobe is tender-hearted, whose thoughts are like water,
yielding to everything, and nothing to be seen.

Ceres. Well, let us to Cupid. And take heed that in your stub-   85
bornness you offend him not, whom by entreaties you
ought to follow. Diana's nymphs were as chaste as Ceres'
virgins, as fair, as wise. How Cupid tormented them I
had rather you should hear than feel; but this is truth,
they all yielded to love. [*They regard her incredulously.*]   90
Look not scornfully, my nymphs; I say they are yielded
to love. [*They come to a halt before the temple of Cupid.*]
This is the temple. – Thou great god, Cupid, whom the

76–8. conceits . . . but certainly] *Punctuation this ed.;* conceites, betwixt
both, a kind of yeelding; I know not what. But certainely *Q;* conceits;
betwixt both, a kind of yeilding; I know not what. But certainely *Fairholt;*
conceits, betwixt both a kind of yielding; I know not what, but certainly
Edge; conceits; betwixt both a kind of yielding, I know not what. But
certainly *Daniel.* 79. smile] *Q;* smite *Daniel.* 80. heat] *Q;* heart
Edge. 90. SD] *This ed.* 92. SD] *This ed.*

---

74. *felt him*] experienced his power.

76. *hard conceits*] cruel fancies.

78. *ease*] relief.

80–2. *I feel . . . hate*] Compare Cupid's description of love in *Galatea*: 'A
heat full of coldness, a sweet full of bitterness, a pain full of pleasantness'
(1.2.18–19). The paradoxical nature of love is a pervasive motif in the Lylian
corpus.

85. *let us to*] let us go to. For the implied SD here see line 46 SDn. above.

85–6. *stubbornness*] obduracy.

86–7. *by entreaties . . . follow*] you should follow with prayers.

87–90. *Diana's nymphs . . . to love*] The reference is to the action of
Galatea, in which Diana's nymphs (Telusa, Ramia, and Eurota) all fall victim
to love through Cupid's agency.

gods regard and men reverence, let it be lawful for Ceres
to offer her sacrifice.   95

[*Enter* CUPID *from his temple.*]

Cupid. Divine Ceres, Cupid accepteth anything that cometh
from Ceres, which feedeth my sparrows with ripe corn,
my pigeons with wholesome seeds, and honourest my
temple with chaste virgins.

Ceres. [*Offering doves*] Then, Love, to thee I bring these white   100
and spotless doves, in token that my heart is as free from
any thought of love as these from any blemish, and as
clear in virginity as these perfect in whiteness. But that
my nymphs may know both thy power and thy laws, and
neither err in ignorance nor pride, let me ask some ques-   105
tions to instruct them, that they offend not thee, whom
resist they cannot. In virgins, what dost thou chiefest
desire?

Cupid. In those that are not in love, reverent thoughts of love;
in those that be, faithful vows.   110

Ceres. What dost thou most hate in virgins?

Cupid. Pride in the beautiful, bitter taunts in the witty, incredulity in all.

95.1. SD] *This ed.; The temple-doors open. / Bond (following line 93 this ed.,*
'This is the temple'.*); The temple doors open, revealing* Cupid. / *Edge (positioning as Bond); Enter* CUPID. / *Daniel (positioning as this ed.).*   100. SD] *This ed.*

94. *regard*] respect.
97–8. *sparrows . . . pigeons*] both traditionally associated with aspects of
love. Sparrows, emblematic of the sexual appetite, drew the carriage of
Aphrodite (Venus), while pigeons (i.e. doves) are among the cluster of birds
sacred to Cupid. (See also 1.2.66n.)
100–1. *I bring . . . doves*] Though Nisa indicates at 1.2.66 that Ceres is in
the habit of presenting an eagle to Cupid as well as a pair of doves, there is
no textual indication that she does so in the course of this scene.
103. *clear*] unspotted, immaculate. Compare *Mac.*: 'This Duncan
/ . . . hath been / So clear in his great office' (1.7.16–18).
107–33.] The exchange constitutes a species of catechism designed to
instruct not the respondent but the attendant nymphs. For further instances
of the highly patterned stichomythic dialogue recurrent throughout the play
see 3.1.88–93 and 3.1.108ff.
112–13.] The qualities most offensive to Cupid are those which conventionally characterized the Petrarchan mistress, and which are exhibited by
the three nymphs.
incredulity] disbelief.

Ceres. What may protect my virgins that they may never
    love?   115
Cupid. That they be never idle.
Ceres. Why didst thou so cruelly torment all Diana's nymphs
    with love?
Cupid. Because they thought it impossible to love.
Ceres. What is the substance of love?   120
Cupid. Constancy and secrecy.
Ceres. What the signs?
Cupid. Sighs and tears.
Ceres. What the causes?
Cupid. Wit and idleness.   125
Ceres. What the means?
Cupid. Opportunity and importunity.
Ceres. What the end?
Cupid. Happiness without end.
Ceres. What requirest thou of men?   130
Cupid. That only shall be known to men.
Ceres. What revenge for those that will not love?
Cupid. To be deceived when they do.

114–16.] See 1.2.51–2n.

117–18.] The question again alludes to the passions Cupid induced in
Diana's followers in *Galatea*. See 2.1. 87–90n.

120. *substance*] essence.

121. *secrecy*] Ovid contends in *Rem. am.* that secrecy heightens passion
(line 581).

123.] Compare Sylvius' description of love in *AYL*: 'It is to be all made
of sighs and tears' (5.2.82). Lyly is drawing here on *Ars am.*, i, 659–60.

124–7. *What the causes . . . importunity*] The exchange is summarized,
rather than quoted directly, by Pudsey: 'The causes of loue witt and Idlenes,
ye meanes opportunitye & imp<er>tunitye' (86v).

125. *Wit*] The association between wit and love is played out in *Anatomy*
through the relationship between Euphues, Philautus, and Lucilla.

127. *Opportunity*] Compare the advice offered by a courtier to Fidus
in *England*: 'When I [Fidus] demanded what was the first thing to win my
lady, he answered, "Opportunity," asking what was the second, he said,
"Opportunity," desirous to know what might be the third, he replied,
"Opportunity" ' (p. 201).

importunity] constant solicititation.

128. *end*] goal.

131. *only shall*] shall only.

Ceres. Well, Cupid, entreat my nymphs with favour, and,
 though to love it be no vice, yet spotless virginity is the   135
 only virtue. Let me keep their thoughts as chaste as their
 bodies, that Ceres may be happy, and they praised.
Cupid. Why, Ceres, do you think that lust followeth love?
 Ceres, lovers are chaste! For what is love, divine love, but
 the quintessence of chastity, and affections binding by   140
 heavenly motions, that cannot be undone by earthly
 means, and must not be controlled by any man?
Ceres. We will honour thee with continual sacrifice. Warm us
 with mild affections, lest being too hot, we seem immod-
 est, like wantons, or too cold, immovable, like stocks.   145
Cupid. Ceres, let this serve for all. Let not thy nymphs be
 light, nor obstinate, but, as virgins should be, pitiful and
 faithful. So shall your flames warm, but not burn; delight,
 and never discomfort.   [*Exit.*]

---

149. SD] *This ed.*

134. *entreat . . . favour*] behave favourably to my nymphs.

138. *Why, Ceres . . . followeth love*] For the nature of the love Cupid
embodies see Introduction, pp. 24ff. above.

139. *lovers are chaste*] The same concept is implicit in the first question
posed by Venus to the lovers of *Galatea* before she agrees to facilitate their
union: 'Is your loves unspotted?' (5.3.145–6).

140. *quintessence*] purest and most refined form.

140–1. *affections . . . motions*] passions made binding through the opera-
tions of the spirit.

141–2. *cannot be . . . means*] Compare Cupid's inability in *Galatea* to untie
a love knot 'knit by faith' which can 'only be unknit of death' (4.2.50–1).

145. *or too*] or being too.

immovable] we seem incapable of feeling (*OED* a. 2c).

stocks] (*a*) tree stumps; (*b*) stoics. Lyly employs the same pun in *Anatomy*
on more than one occasion, cf.: 'Who so severe as the Stoics, which like
stocks were moved with no melody' (p. 38). See also *Shrew*: 'Let's be no
stoics nor no stocks, I pray' (1.1.31).

147. *light*] easily won, frivolous.

pitiful] compassionate.

148. *your flames*] the passions you experience.

149. *discomfort*] cause distress.

149. SD] Cupid's exit at this point may be inferred from the fact that
Ceres addresses her last speech exclusively to her nymphs and returns at the
close to a matter with which Cupid is not yet concerned.

Ceres. How say you, my nymphs, doth not Cupid speak like   150
   a god? Counsel you, I will not, to love; but conjure you,
   I must, that you be not disdainful. Let us in, and see how
   Erisichthon speedeth. Famine flieth swiftly, and hath
   already seized on his stomach.   *Exeunt.*

---

151. you, I will not, to] *Punctuation this ed.;* you I will not to *Q;* you I will,
not to *Daniel.*

151-2. *Counsel you . . . disdainful*] Whereas Daniel's introduction of a
comma after 'will' in 151 (see collation note) changes the force of Ceres'
closing remarks, the punctuation adopted here is designed to heighten the
parallel between the two halves of the sentence, while clarifying the sense of
the lighter pointing of *Q.*
   151. *conjure*] solemnly call upon, earnestly exhort.
   153. *speedeth*] is faring.

Act 3

[*Enter*] NISA, [*pursued by*] RAMIS.

Ramis. Stay, cruel Nisa! Thou knowest not from whom thou
    fliest, and therefore fliest. I come not to offer violence,
    but that which is inviolable. My thoughts are as holy as
    thy vows, and I as constant in love as thou in cruelty.
    Lust followeth not my love as shadows do bodies, but   5
    truth is woven into my love as veins into bodies. Let me
    touch this tender arm, and say my love is endless.
Nisa. And to no end.
Ramis. It is without spot.
Nisa. And shall be without hope.   10
Ramis. Dost thou disdain Love and his laws?
Nisa. I do not disdain that which I think is not, yet laugh at
    those that honour it if it be.

3.1.0. Actus tertius, Scena prima] *Q;* [III,i.] *Edge;* Act 3 SCENE 1 *Daniel.*
Bond supplies <*A Glade in the Forest, with transfer to the Tree,* l. 157.> *(error*
for 155, line 170 this ed.). 0.1. SD] *This ed.; Ramis, Nisa, Montanus, Celia,*
Siluestris, Niobe. / *Q;* RAMIS, NISA, MONTANUS, CELIA, SILUESTRIS, NIOBE.
<*Enter* RAMIS, *pursuing* NISA.> / *Bond;* [*Enter*] Ramis, [*pursuing*] Nisa. / *Edge;*
Enter RAMIS *and* NISA. / *Daniel.*

3.1.0.1] Though *Q* lists all the characters who appear in the scene at the
outset, it is clear from the sequential exchanges between the lovers, and the
'*Exeunt*' marked at line 39, that the lovers exit and enter in pairs.
    1–2. *Thou knowest . . . fliest*] The words are based on Apollo's appeal to
Daphne when pursuing her in Ovid, *Met.*, bk i: 'Thou doest not know poore
simple soule, God wote thou dost not knowe, / From whome thou fleest.
For if thou knew, thou wouldste not flee me so' (625–6 / LCL 514–15).
    3. *that which is inviolable*] i.e. faithful love.
    5. *Lust . . . love*] The declaration accords with Cupid's contention at
2.1.139 that 'lovers are chaste'.
    8. *to no end*] pointless, in vain.
    12–13.] The assertion places Nisa in direct opposition to Cupid, who has
indicated in 2.1 that one of the qualities he 'most hate[s] in virgins' is
'incredulity' (lines 111–13).

Ramis. Time shall bring to pass that Nisa shall confess there
  is love.   15
Nisa. Then also will love make me confess that Nisa is a
  fool.
Ramis. Is it folly to love, which the gods account honourable,
  and men esteem holy?
Nisa. The gods make anything lawful, because they be gods;   20
  and men honour shadows for substance, because they are
  men.
Ramis. Both gods and men agree that love is a consuming of
  the heart and restoring, a bitter death in a sweet life.
Nisa. Gods do know, and men should, that love is a consum-   25
  ing of wit, and restoring of folly; a staring blindness, and
  a blind gazing.
Ramis. Wouldst thou allot me death?
Nisa. No, but discretion.
Ramis. Yield some hope.   30
Nisa. Hope to despair.
Ramis. Not so long as Nisa is a woman.
Nisa. Therein, Ramis, you show yourself a man.
Ramis. Why?
Nisa. In flattering yourself that all women will yield.   35
Ramis. All may.
Nisa. Thou shalt swear that we cannot.
Ramis. I will follow thee, and practise by denials to be patient,
  or by disdaining die, and so be happy.   *Exeunt.*

---

18. account] *Q* (accompt). *Also at 5.1.46 and 5.4.129.*   24. heart and restoring, a] *Bond;* heart, and restoring a *Q.*   39. SD] *Q;* [*Exeunt.*] *Edge.*

23–4. *a consuming . . . life*] See 2.1.80–2 for a similarly paradoxical definition of love.

26. *staring*] Though implying the capacity to see, the word carries connotations of blindness through its proximity to the now archaic compound
'stareblind' (to be blind without any visible sign of lesion to the eyes). Lyly
uses the same image suggesting the simultaneous distance and proximity
between related states in *Anatomy*, cf.: 'consider with thyself the great
difference between staring and stark-blind, wit and wisdom, love and lust'
(pp. 37–8).

37. *we cannot*] women are incapable of love.

39. *by disdaining die*] die through being subjected to scorn.

[*Enter* CELIA, *pursued by* MONTANUS.]

Montanus. [*Panting*] Though thou hast overtaken me in love,   40
yet have I overtaken thee in running. Fair Celia, yield to
love, to sweet love!

Celia. Montanus, thou art mad, that, having no breath almost
in running so fast, thou wilt yet spend more in speaking
so foolishly. Yield to love I cannot; or if I do, to thy love   45
I will not.

Montanus. The fairest wolf chooseth the foulest, if he be
faithfullest, and he that endureth most grief, not he that
hath most beauty.

Celia. If my thoughts were wolfish, thy hopes might be as thy   50
comparison is, beastly.

Montanus. I would thy words were as thy looks are, lovely.

Celia. I would thy looks were as thy affection is, blind.

Montanus. Fair faces should have smooth hearts.

Celia. Fresh flowers have crooked roots.   55

Montanus. Women's beauties will wane, and then no art can
make them fair.

Celia. Men's follies will ever wax, and then what reason can
make them wise?

Montanus. To be amiable and not to love is, like a painted   60
lady, to have colours and no life.

39.1. SD] *This ed.; Enter* MONTANUS, *pursuing* CELIA. / *Bond; Enter*
MONTANUS *and* CELIA. / *Daniel.*   40. SD] *This ed.*

40–1. *overtaken . . . overtaken*] ensnared (*OED* v. 7) . . . caught (*OED* v. 1).

47–9.] proverbial (Dent, W606.11). Dent cites Pettie, *A Petite Pallace of Pleasure*, 17 (1576): 'The Shee woulfe . . . always chooseth that woulfe for her make [mate] who is made most leane and foule by following her.' Compare *Anatomy*: 'The wolf chooseth him for her make that hath or doth endure most travail for her sake' (p. 82).

50–1.] If my mind functioned on the same level as an animal's, you might have some prospect of achieving the physical relationship your comparison suggests.

54.] The assertion accords with the neoplatonic concept that the face is the mirror of the soul, and that outward beauty correlates with inner worth.

55.] proverbial (Tilley, T511). Lucilla similarly advises Euphues in *Anatomy* that 'the words of men though they seem smooth as oil, yet their hearts are as crooked as the stalk of ivy' (p. 69).

58. *wax*] grow.

60. *amiable*] (*a*) beautiful; (*b*) one who invites love.

Celia. To be amorous and not lovely is, like a pleasant fool,
   full of words and no deserts.
Montanus. What call you deserts? What lovely?
Celia. No lovelier thing than wit; no greater desert than   65
   patience.
Montanus. Have not I an excellent wit?
Celia. If thou think so thyself, thou art an excellent fool.
Montanus. [*Angrily*] Fool? No, Celia, thou shalt find me as
   wise as I do thee proud, and as little to digest thy taunts   70
   as thou to brook my love.
Celia. I thought, Montanus, that you could not deserve, when
   I told you what it was: patience.
Montanus. Sweet Celia, I will be patient, and forget this.
Celia. Then want you wit, that you can be content to be   75
   patient.
Montanus. A hard choice: if I take all well, to be a fool; if find
   fault, then to want patience.
Celia. The fortune of love, and the virtue, is neither to have
   success nor mean. Farewell.   [*Exit.*]   80
Montanus. Farewell? Nay, I will follow! And I know not how
   it cometh to pass, disdain increaseth desire; and the

---

69. SD] *This ed.; with heat | Bond.*   70. digest] *This ed.; disgest Q.*
80. SD] *Bond; Exeunt. | Fairholt.*

62. *lovely*] (*a*) attractive; (*b*) one who invites love.
pleasant] facetious.
63. *deserts*] actions worthy of recompense, merits.
68.] proverbial. Tilley (C582) cites *Love's Metamorphosis* among a number
of other examples, including Sanford's *The Garden of Pleasure* (1573), 'The
greatest token of a foole is to accounte him selfe wise' (f. 51v).
70–1. *little to digest . . . brook*] disinclined to stomach . . . endure.
75. *want*] lack.
77. *take all well*] accept everything you say in good part.
79. *fortune* (*a*) destiny; (*b*) happiness.
virtue] (*a*) particular quality; (*b*) merit.
80. *mean*] (*a*) middle way; (*b*) moderation. Compare *Mother Bombie*:
'Loue and beautie disdaine a meane, not . . . because beautie is no vertue,
but because it is happiness' (2.3.24–6). Bond notes in relation to this passage:
'Lyly is thinking of the Aristotelian doctrine of virtue as a mean between two
vicious extremes, while happiness, the end of virtue . . . is not to be measured
by the same standard of comparison' (iii, p. 543).
82–3. *the further possibility standeth*] the more distant the hope of
success.

further possibility standeth, the nearer approacheth hope.
I follow!   [*Exit.*]

[*Enter* NIOBE, *pursued by* SILVESTRIS.]

Silvestris. Polypus, Niobe, is ever of the colour of the stone it   85
    sticketh to, and thou ever of his humour thou talkest
    with.
Niobe. Find you fault that I love?
Silvestris. So many.
Niobe. Would you have me like none?   90
Silvestris. Yes, one.
Niobe. Who shall make choice but myself?
Silvestris. Myself.
Niobe. For another to put thoughts into my head were to pull
    the brains out of my head. Take not measure of my affec-   95
    tions, but weigh your own. The oak findeth no fault with
    the dew because it also falleth on the bramble. Believe
    me, Silvestris, the only way to be mad is to be constant.

---

84. SD] *Bond; Exeunt.* / *Fairholt.*   84.1. SD] *This ed.; Enter* SILVESTRIS
and NIOBE. / *Bond.*

   85. *Polypus*] fish reputed to adapt its colour to the surrounding environment, and described, as Bond notes (iii, p. 566), by Pliny (*Hist. nat.*, ix, 46).
The immediate source here, however, is probably Erasmus (*Similia*, 585B),
in that a reference to the polypus in *Anatomy* (p. 64) is directly followed, as
in the *Similia*, by an image involving Proteus (see Croll and Clemons,
p. 58n.).
   86. *humour*] frame of mind.
   94–5. *For another . . . out of my head*] The first of three passages in the act
noted by Pudsey. (See also 3.1.99–100 and 3.2.31–2 below.)
   pull . . . head] rob me of my own thoughts.
   96–7. *The oak . . . bramble*] Compare *WT*: 'The selfsame sun that shines
upon his court / Hides not his visage from our cottage' (4.4.446–7). No
other example of Lyly's version of the proverb (Tilley, S985) has been
traced.
   97. *dew*] commonly associated with divine benevolence (cf. *H8*, 4.2.133:
'The dews of heaven fall thick in blessings on her').
   98. *the only way . . . constant*] Edge cites Tilley, M978, 'You will never be
mad (married), you are of so many minds', and suggests that a portmanteau
pun may be involved here: 'mad = (1) inconstant, (2) maid, (3) married'
(p. 644). The assertion may merely be a variant, however, on the paradox
repeatedly enforced in Lyly's work that the only constant is inconstancy
(i.e. if I were constant to one it would make me unstable).

Poets make their wreaths of laurel, ladies of sundry
flowers.   100

Silvestris. Sweet Niobe, a river running into divers brooks
becometh shallow, and a mind divided into sundry affections in the end will have none. What joy can I take in
the fortune of my love, when I shall know many to have
the like favours? Turtles flock by couples, and breed both   105
joy and young ones.

Niobe. But bees in swarms, and bring forth wax and honey.

Silvestris. Why do you covet many, that may find sweetness
in one?

Niobe. Why had Argus an hundred eyes, and might have seen   110
with one?

Silvestris. Because whilst he slept with some, he might wake
with other some.

Niobe. And I love many, because being deceived by the inconstancy of divers, I might yet have one.   115

Silvestris. That was but a device of Juno, that knew Jupiter's
love.

Niobe. And this a rule of Venus, that knew men's lightness.

Silvestris. The whole heaven hath but one sun.

99–100. *Poets . . . flowers*] Compare *England*: '[ladies] take more delight
to gather flowers one by one in a garden than to snatch them by handfuls
from a garland' (p. 161). A chaplet of laurel was awarded in ancient Rome
to those who distinguished themselves in the poetic arts. The analogy is
among the passages noted by Pudsey.

99. *sundry*] a variety of.

101–2. *a river . . . shallow*] proverbial (Tilley, R139). Lyly's immediate
source may have been Erasmus (*Similia*, 584D).

101. *divers*] several. (See also line 115 below.)

105. *favours*] signs of approbation of a suit (often in the form of the
bestowal of a token, e.g. a glove).

Turtles] turtle doves. (See 1.2.66n.)

108. *covet*] desire.

110. *Argus*] See 2.1.69n.

112–13. *wake . . . other some*] keep watch (*OED* v. I 2) . . . others.

115. *yet*] still.

116–17. See 2.1.69n.

118. *this . . . lightness*] my conduct . . . inconstancy.

119–38.] Edge notes: 'Friederich Brie, in his article "Lyly und Greene"
in *Englische Studien*, XLII (1910), 217–222, compares Greene's *Alcida*: "for
wee see that in the firmament there is but one sunne: yea, quoth *Eriphila*,
but there be many stars. The Iris or Rainbow Madam (qd. he) hath but one

Niobe. But stars infinite.   120

Silvestris. The rainbow is ever in one compass.

Niobe. But of sundry colours.

Silvestris. A woman hath but one heart.

Niobe. But a thousand thoughts.

Silvestris. My lute, though it have many strings, maketh a   125
    sweet consent; and a lady's heart, though it harbour
    many fancies, should embrace but one love.

Niobe. The strings of my heart are tuned in a contrary key to
    your lute, and make as sweet harmony in discords as
    yours in concord.   130

Silvestris. Why, what strings are in ladies' hearts? Not the
    bass?

Niobe. There is no base string in a woman's heart.

Silvestris. The mean?

Niobe. There was never mean in woman's heart.   135

---

132. bass] *Daniel;* base *Q, Bond, Fairholt, Edge.*

---

quality. Truth answered my daughter, but it hath many colours: but to come
to a familiar example, replyed *Meribates*: the heart hath but one string; yea
but, quoth *Eriphila*, it hath many thoughts" . . . Brie sees this as evidence for
the position that Lyly took the nymph-foresters plot from Greene' (p. 645).
For a discussion of the significance of this contention in relation to the
history of the play see Introduction, p. 7. The fascination with the union of
opposites (in this instance, one encompassing many) is evident throughout
Lyly's work.

   120. *stars infinite*] an infinite number of stars.

   121. *compass*] curve (*OED* sb[1]. IV6).

   125–38.] The interrelated musical metaphors here all occur elsewhere in
Lyly's work. The notion of the tuning of discordant strings to produce
harmony is used, for example, in *England* in the context of a disrupted
friendship (cf. 'Friends must be used as the musicians tune their strings,
who finding them in a discord do not break them, but either by intention
or remission frame them to a pleasant consent': p. 285), while the pun on
bass, mean, and treble voices occurs in an exchange between Venus and the
would-be apprentices of *Galatea* (cf. '*Venus.* Can you sing? / *Rafe.* Basely. /
Venus. And you? / *Dick.* Meanly. / *Venus.* And what can you do? / *Robin.* If
they double it, I will treble it': 5.3.201–6). For a comparable play on the
strings of an instrument and heart strings see *TGV*, 4.2. 54–60. The notion
of *concordia discors* (harmony in discord) is a Renaissance commonplace.

   126. *consent*] harmony.

   132, 133. *bass . . . base*] lowest part in a song for three voices . . . morally
low.

   134, 135. *mean . . . mean*] middle part in a song for three voices . . .
spiritual ungenerosity.

Silvestris. The treble?

Niobe. Yea, the treble – double and treble; and so are all my
heart strings. Farewell!

Silvestris. [*Detaining her*] Sweet Niobe, let us sing, that I may
die with the swan.   140

Niobe. It will make you sigh the more, and live with the
salamich.

Silvestris. Are thy tunes fire?

Niobe. Are yours death?

Silvestris. No; but when I have heard thy voice, I am content   145
to die.

Niobe. I will sing to content thee.

　　　　　　　　　Cantant. [*Exit* NIOBE *following the song.*]

Silvestris. Inconstant Niobe! Unhappy Silvestris! Yet had I
rather she should rather love all than none; for now,
though I have no certainty, yet do I find a kind of   150
sweetness.

---

139. SD] *This ed.*   147.1. SD] *Bracketed material this ed.; Cantant.* / *Q;
Cantant <then exit* NIOBE.> / *Bond; They sing. After the song, exit* NIOBE. /
Daniel.

136, 137. *treble . . . treble*] highest   part   in   a   song   for   three
voices . . . triple.

139–40. *let us . . . swan*] Swans, mute during life, were reputed to sing on
the point of death (cf. *Sappho and Phao*: 'Swans that end their lives with
songs are covered when they are dead with flowers': 2.4.35–6). Ovid draws
on the myth in *Met.*, bk xiv (485–7 / LCL 428–30).

142. *salamich*] salamander. Edge (p. 645) identifies the salamich with
both the mythical creature, alluded to by Ovid (*Met.*, bk xv, 453–4 / LCL
411–12), capable of living on air (hence 'sigh the more'), and the salamander
(p. 646) capable of living in fire (hence 'Are thy tunes fire?': line 117). It was
the chameleon, however, not the salamander that was thought to be capable
of living on air, as Lyly was plainly aware (cf. 'Love is a chameleon, which
draweth nothing into the mouth but air': *Endymion*, 3.4.136–7), and there is
no evidence to suggest that the two creatures were ever conflated. Rather
than suggesting the capacity to live on air, 'sigh the more' probably signifies
fall more deeply in love (i.e. burn in the flames of passion), and hence 'live
with the salamich', i.e. the salamander. 'Salamich' is not recorded in the
OED, but seems unlikely to have been Lyly's invention, given that he uses
the term 'salamander' elsewhere (cf. *Anatomy*, p. 64).

144. *Are yours death?*] The question looks back to lines 139–40 in which
Silvestris expresses his desire to die as they sing.

147.1. Cantant] The song indicated here has not been preserved.

[*Enter* RAMIS.]

Ramis. Cruel Nisa, born to slaughter men!

[*Enter* MONTANUS.]

Montanus. Coy Celia, bred up in scoffs!

Silvestris. Wavering, yet witty, Niobe! But are we all met?

Ramis. Yea, and met withal, if your fortunes be answerable   155
    to mine; for I find my mistress immovable, and the hope
    I have is to despair.

Montanus. Mine in pride intolerable, who biddeth me look
    for no other comfort than contempt.

Silvestris. Mine is best of all, and worst. This is my hope, that   160
    either she will have many or none.

Ramis. I fear our fortunes cannot thrive, for Erisichthon hath
    felled down the holy tree of Ceres, which will increase in
    her choler, and in her nymphs cruelty. Let us see whether
    our garlands be there which we hanged on that tree, and   165
    let us hang ourselves upon another.

Silvestris. A remedy for love irremovable. But I will first see
    whether all those that love Niobe do like. In the mean
    season, I will content myself with my share.

151.1. SD] *Daniel; Re-enter* RAMIS. / *Bond.*   152.1. SD] *Daniel; Re-enter*
MONTANUS. / *Bond.*   165. that] *Q;* the *Fairholt.*

154, 155. *met . . . met*] gathered together . . . confounded.

155–6. *be answerable to*] agree with.

156. *immovable*] incapable of being emotionally stirred.

163–4. *increase in her choler*] heighten anger in her.

164. *Let us see*] an implied stage direction signalling a movement to the
site of Ceres' grove.

165. *garlands*] See 1.1.02n.

166. *hang ourselves*] Suicide by hanging was traditionally regarded as a
product of despair echoing the death of Judas on an elder tree. The word-
play ('we hanged' / 'hang ourselves') is characteristically Lylian.

167. *A remedy . . . irremovable*] An appropriate cure for an ineradicable
attachment.

167–9. *But I . . . share*] The lines indicate that Niobe and Silvestris are
well matched in terms of temperament, in that, whereas Ramis is ready to
die for love, Silvestris is prepared to temporize and accept a share of Niobe's
affections in the hope that his rivals will hang themselves first.

168–9. *mean season*] meantime.

Montanus. Here is the tree. [*He sees the destruction wrought by*   170
    Erisichthon.] Oh, mischief scarce to be believed; impossi-
    ble to be pardoned!

Ramis. Pardoned it is not, for Erisichthon perisheth with
    famine, and is able to starve those that look on him. Here
    hang our garlands. [*He sees the inscriptions.*] Something is   175
    written. [*To Silvestris*] Read mine.

Silvestris. [*Taking up the first inscription*] 'Cedit amor rebus, res
    age tutus eris.'

Montanus. And mine.

Silvestris. [*Taking up the second inscription*] 'Sat mihi si facies,   180
    sit bene nota mihi.' Now for myself. [*He takes up the third
    inscription.*] 'Victoria tecum stabit.' Scilicet!

Montanus. You see their posies is as their hearts, and their
    hearts as their speeches: cruel, proud, and wavering. Let
    us all to the temple of Cupid and entreat his favour, if   185
    not to obtain their loves, yet to revenge their hates. Cupid
    is a kind god, who, knowing our unspotted thoughts, will
    punish them, or release us. We will study what revenge
    to have, that our pains proceeding of our own minds,
    their plagues may also proceed from theirs. Are you all   190
    agreed?

170–1, 175, 176, 177, 180, 181–2. SD] *All bracketed material this
ed.*   182. *stabit.*' Scilicet!] *This ed.; stabit scilicet. / Q; stabit – scilicet. / Bond
(noting 'scilicet as part of quotation Q F').*

---

170. *Here is the tree*] See line 164n. above.

177–82. Cedit amor . . . stabit] See 1.2. 51–2, 55, and 60nn. for transla-
tions of the three Latin inscriptions.

182. *Scilicet!*] Naturally! Daniel assumes (p. 382) that the exclamation is
the concluding word of the inscription, but this is not borne out by 1.2.60
in which Niobe reads her response to Silvestris aloud. Rather than being
part of Niobe's reply, the exclamation is more likely to be an ironic comment
by Silvestris on her response to his suit. He will be successful to the extent
that all her lovers are successful. Lyly uses the same exclamation in close
proximity to the concept of hanging for love in *Midas* (1.2.39–40).

183. *posies*] mottoes. The seeming lack of agreement with the verb that
follows indicates that Montanus sees the nymphs' posies as a single item,
indicative of their stance.

189–90. *our pains . . . theirs*] just as our pangs derive from our mental
states, their sufferings may be a product of their own natures.

Silvestris. I consent. But what if Cupid deny help?

Montanus. Then he is no god.

Silvestris. But if he yield, what shall we ask?

Ramis. Revenge.   195

Montanus. Then let us prepare ourselves for Cupid's sacrifice.

                                        Exeunt.

                Actus tertius, Scena secunda

        [*Enter*] ERISICHTHON, [*emaciated with hunger, and*]
                        PROTEA.

Erisichthon. Come, Protea, dear daughter; that name must
    thou buy too dear. Necessity causeth thee to be sold;
    nature must frame thee to be contented. Thou see'st in
    how short a space I have turned all my goods into my
    guts, where I feel a continual fire which nothing can   5
    quench. My famine increaseth by eating, resembling the

3.2.0. Actus tertius, Scena secunda] *Q;* SCENA SECUNDA. – <*Seashore near*
ERISICHTHON'S *Farm.*> / *Bond;* [III,ii.] *Edge;* SCENE 2 *Daniel.*   0.1–2. SD.
[*Enter . . .* PROTEA.] *This ed.; Erisicthon, Protea, Marchant.* / *Q;* ERISCTHON,
PROTEA, MARCHANT. <*Enter* ERISICHTHON *and* PROTEA.> / *Bond;* [*Enter*]
Erisichthon, Protea. *Edge.*

───

3.2.0.1. SD. emaciated with hunger] The fact that Erisichthon has been
physically changed by his insatiable hunger is indicated at 5.4.16–17 when
Ceres, having remitted his punishment, presents him to Cupid (cf. 'Cupid,
here is Erisichthon in his former state; restore my nymphs to theirs').
    1. *that name*] the title of daughter. Edge assumes that Erisichthon is allud-
ing to the meaning of the name 'Protea' and the fact that he 'plans to sell
her, whilst she is in varying shapes, to different buyers' (p. 647), but it is
clear from 4.2.1–2 that he has no knowledge of how she escapes the Merchant. The fact that Protea asks her father to withdraw while she prays to
Neptune (3.2.21–3) is indicative of his ignorance of her intentions, while in
the Ovidian source it is Protea who envisages the possibility of escape (cf.:
Met., bk viii, 1052ff. / LCL 848ff.). It is only when her father is told, in the
poem, how she has eluded the Merchant that he plans to sell her over and
over again (cf. *Met.*, bk viii, 1079–83 / LCL 871–4).
    3. *nature*] the natural bond between father and daughter.
    frame] make.
    6–7. *My famine . . . filled*] Tilley (S181) cites the lines as an example of
the proverb 'The sea refuses no river (is never full)'. Compare *TN*: 'O spirit
of love, how quick and fresh art thou, / That notwithstanding thy capacity
/ Receiveth as the sea, nought enters there, / Of what validity and pitch
soe'er, / But falls into abatement and low price, / Even in a minute!'
(1.1.9–14).

sea, which receiveth all things and cannot be filled. Life
is sweet, hunger sharp; between them the contention
must be short, unless thou, Protea, prolong it. I have
acknowledged my offence against Ceres; make amends I   10
cannot. For the gods holding the balance in their hands,
what recompense can equally weigh with their punishments? Or what is he, that having but one ill thought of
Ceres, that can raze it with a thousand dutiful actions?
Such is the difference that none can find defence. This   15
is the odds: we miserable, and men; they immortal, and
gods.

Protea. Dear father, I will obey both to sale and slaughter,
accounting it the only happiness of my life, should I live
an hundred years, to prolong yours but one minute. I   20
yield, father. Chop and change me, I am ready. But first,
let me make my prayers to Neptune, and withdraw yourself till I have done. Long it shall not be; now it must
be.

Erisichthon. Stay, sweet Protea, and that great god hear thy   25
prayer, though Ceres stop her ears to mine.

                              [*He stands aside.*]

Protea. [*Praying*] Sacred Neptune, whose godhead conquered
my maidenhead, be as ready to hear my passions as I was
to believe thine, and perform that now, I entreat, which
thou didst promise when thyself didst love. Let not me   30

---

14. raze] *This ed.;* race *Q;* 'race *Fairholt;* rase *Edge.*   19. accounting] *Q*
(*accompting*).   26.1. SD] *This ed.;* ERISICHTHON retires. / *Bond; Retires.* /
Edge.   27. SD] *This ed.*

7–8. *Life . . . sharp*] both proverbial (Tilley, L254 and H818: 'Hunger is
sharper than thorn').

11. *balance*] scales (of justice).

14. *that can*] can (with 'that' repeated pleonastically from 'that having' in
line 13).

raze] obliterate.

16. *odds*] balance of advantage (cf. *Tit.*: 'Thou hast the odds of me':
5.2.19).

21. *Chop and change*] Exchange (Tilley, C363).

25. *and that*] and may that.

26. *stop*] close.

28. *passions*] (*a*) lamentations; (*b*) amatory feelings (cf. *Tit.*: (*a*) 'A
mother's tears in passion for her son' (1.1.109); (*b*) 'And plead my passions
for Lavinia's love' (2.1.36)).

be a prey to this Merchant, who knows no other god than
gold, unless it be falsely swearing by a god to get gold.
Let me, as often as I be bought for money or pawned for
meat, be turned into a bird, hare, or lamb, or any shape
wherein I may be safe. So shall I preserve mine own   35
honour, my father's life, and never repent me of thy love.
And now, bestir thee, for of all men I hate that Merchant,
who, if he find my beauty worth one penny, will put it to
use to gain ten, having no religion in his mind, nor word
in his mouth, but money. Neptune, hear now, or never!   40
– Father, I have done.

Erisichthon. [*Coming forward*] In good time, Protea, thou hast
done; for lo, the Merchant keepeth not only day, but
hour.

[*Enter the* MERCHANT.]

Protea. [*Aside to her father*] If I had not been here, had I been   45
forfeited?

Erisichthon. [*Aside to Protea*] No, Protea, but thy father famished. [*To the Merchant*] Here, gentleman, I am ready
with my daughter.

Protea. Gentleman?   50

---

42. SD] *Bond (subst.)*.   44.1. SD] *Daniel (subst.); Enter a* Merchant. /
Bond, Edge (following famished, *lines 47–8 this ed.*).   45, 47, 48. SD] *All
bracketed material this ed.*

31–2. *Merchant . . . get gold*] The passage is noted by Pudsey.

34. *meat*] food.

bird . . . any shape] Compare *Met.*, bk. viii, 1081–3 / LCL 873–4: 'now a
Mare, / And now a Cow, and now a Bird, a Hart, a Hynd, or Hare, /
[She]ever fed her hungry Syre with undeserved fare'.

37. *bestir thee*] act quickly.

38–9. *put it to use*] employ it (*a*) for commercial advantage; (*b*) for the
purposes of usury; (*c*) for sexual purposes.

41. *done*] finished.

43–4. *keepeth . . . hour*] keeps his appointment not only to the day but to
the precise time.

45–6.] Would I have been sold had I not been here?

48, 50, 51. *gentleman*] Protea objects to the term of address in that the
Merchant does not belong to the gentry by virtue of birth but has made his
fortune through trade. The Merchant retorts that his 'conditions' (i.e. his
style of life) entitles him to be regarded as a gentleman.

Merchant. Yea, gentleman, fair maid. My conditions make
    me no less.
Protea. Your conditions, indeed, brought in your obligations;
    your obligations, your usury; your usury, your gentry.
Merchant. Why, do you judge no merchants gentlemen?   55
Protea. Yes, many; and some no men.
Merchant. You shall be well entreated at my hands.
Protea. It may. Commanded I will not be.
Merchant. If you be mine by bargain, you shall.
Protea. Father, hath this Merchant also bought my mind?   60
Erisichthon. He cannot buy that which cannot be sold.
Merchant. Here is the money.
Erisichthon. Here the maid. – Farewell, my sweet daughter. I
    commit thee to the gods, and this man's courtesy, who,
    I hope, will deal no worse with thee than he would have   65
    the gods with him. I must be gone, lest I do starve as I
    stand.   *Exit.*

---

53. indeed] *Fairholt, Daniel;* in deed *Q, Bond, Edge.*

53–4.] As Fairholt points out, Protea's response is 'a satirical allusion to
the wording of old bonds, which began with "The condition of this obligation" ' (ii, p. 284). The double meaning of 'conditions' (style of life; terms
of a contract) allows her to retort that it is the crippling 'conditions' imposed
on those who have had dealings with the Merchant that have allowed his
practice of usury to flourish, and his wealth to increase, leading to his claim
to be regarded as a gentleman. The practice of usury was deplored in the
sixteenth century, a period that witnessed increasing pressure on the old
social order through the upward mobility of an increasingly affluent merchant class.

56. *Yes, many*] Protea's response to the Merchant's question again
depends on a pun, here upon the meaning of 'gentleman', i.e. (*a*) a member
of the gentry (the meaning intended by the Merchant); (*b*) one capable of
noble conduct (Protea's meaning).

no men] on a level with beasts.

57. *well entreated ... hands*] (*a*) treated well by me (the Merchant's
meaning in line 57); (*b*) beseeched by me (Protea's meaning in line 58).

58. *It may*] That may be the case.

58–61. *Commanded ... sold*] The lines echo an exchange on personal
liberty in *Campaspe*, cf: '*Parmenio.* Madam, you need not doubt; it is Alexander that is the conqueror. / *Timoclea.* Alexander hath overcome, not conquered. / *Parmenio.* To bring all under his subjection is to conquer. / *Timoclea.*
He cannot subdue that which is divine. / *Parmenio.* Thebes was not. /
Timoclea. Virtue is' (1.1.50–6).

66–7. *as I stand*] even as I stand here.

Protea. Farewell, dear father. I will not cease continually to
    pray to Ceres for thy recovery.
Merchant. You are now mine, Protea.   70
Protea. And mine own.
Merchant. In will, not power.
Protea. In power, if I will.
Merchant. I perceive nettles, gently touched, sting; but,
    roughly handled, make no smart.   75
Protea. Yet, roughly handled, nettles are nettles; and a wasp
    is a wasp, though she lose her sting.
Merchant. But then they do no harm.
Protea. Nor good.
Merchant. Come with me, and you shall see that merchants   80
    know their good as well as gentlemen.
Protea. Sure I am they have gentlemen's goods.   *Exeunt.*

---

69. thy] *Q; not in Fairholt.*

70–3.] See lines 58–61n. above.

72–3.] The lines again echo a punning exchange on the limitations of
power in *Campaspe,* cf. '*Alexander.* Thou shalt live no longer than I will. /
Diogenes. But I shall die whether you will or no' (2.2.163–4).

74–5.] proverbial (Tilley, N133). Compare *Anatomy*: 'he which toucheth
the nettle tenderly is soonest stung' (p. 58).

75. *make no smart*] cause no pain.

81. *know their good*] understand courteous behaviour. Compare Euphues's
response to a gentle reproof in *England*: 'Euphues, as one that knew his good,
answered her in this wise' (p. 297).

82.] The comment is a further sardonic reflection on the transfer of wealth
during the period from the gentry to the merchant class (often through the
mortgaging of lands and possessions).

Act 4

Actus quartus, Scena prima

[*Enter*] RAMIS, MONTANUS, [*and*] SILVESTRIS [*with offerings*].

Ramis. This is the temple of our great god. Let us offer our
sacrifice.

Montanus. I am ready.

Silvestris. And I. – Cupid, thou god of love, whose arrows
have pierced our hearts, give ear to our plaints.   5

[*Enter* CUPID *from his temple.*]

Cupid. If you come to Cupid, speak boldly, so must lovers;
speak faithfully, so must speeders.

Ramis. These ever-burning lamps are signs of my never-to-
be-quenched flames; this bleeding heart, in which yet
sticks the head of the golden shaft, is the lively picture of   10
inward torments. Mine eyes shall bedew thine altars with
tears, and my sighs cover thy temple with a dark smoke.
Pity poor Ramis!   [*He presents his offerings.*]

4.1.0. Actus . . . prima] *Q;* [IV,i.] *Edge;* Act 4 SCENE 1 *Daniel. Bond supplies*
<*Before the Temple of* CUPID.>. 0.1. SD] *Edge (subst.); Ramis, Montanus,
Siluestris, Cupid.* / *Q;* RAMIS, MONTANUS, SILUESTRIS, CUPID. <*Enter the
three* Foresters *with offerings.*> / *Bond; Enter* RAMIS, MONTANUS *and*
SILVESTRIS. / *Daniel.* 5.1. SD] *This ed.; The temple-doors open.* / *Bond;
Enter* CUPID. / *Daniel.* 13. SD] *This ed.*

4.1.1. *our great god*] The description of Cupid as a 'great god' again runs
counter to his presentation in Lyly's previous plays (cf. *Galatea*, 1.2.32).

5. *plaints*] lamentations.

7. *speak faithfully . . . speeders*] Compare Tilley, S719: 'Speak and speed,
ask and have.'

speeders] those who would be successful.

10. *golden shaft*] Cupid was thought to carry arrows of two kinds in his
quiver, some of gold which induced love, and some of lead which repelled
it. Compare Ovid, *Met.*: 'from hys quiver full of shafts two arrowes did he
take / Of sundrie workes: tone causeth Love, the tother doth it slake. / That
causeth love, is all of golde with point full sharpe and bright, / That chaseth
love is blunt, whose steele with leaden head is dight' (bk i, 565–8 / LCL
468–71).

Montanus. With this distaff have I spun, that my exercises
may be as womanish as my affections; and so did Her-   15
cules. And with this halter will I hang myself, if my fortunes answer not my deserts; and so did Iphis. To thee,
divine Cupid, I present not a bleeding but a bloodless
heart, dried only with sorrow and worn with faithful
service. This picture I offer, carved with no other instru-   20
ment than love. Pity poor Montanus!
                              [*He presents his offerings.*]
Silvestris. This fan of swans' and turtles' feathers is token of
my truth and jealousy: jealousy, without which love is
dotage, and with which love is madness; without the
which love is lust, and with which love is folly. This heart,   25
neither bleeding nor bloodless, but swollen with sighs, I
offer to thy godhead, protesting that all my thoughts are,
as my words, without lust, and all my love, as my fortune,
without sweetness. This garland of flowers, which hath
all colours of the rainbow, witnesseth that my heart hath   30
all torments of the world. Pity poor Silvestris!
                              [*He presents his offerings.*]

15. may] *Q; not in Fairholt, Bond.*   21.1, 31.1. SD] *This ed.*

14–16. *With this . . . Hercules*] Sold to Omphale, the daughter of a Lydian
king, in order to expiate an unwitting murder, Hercules fell in love with his
mistress, and spun wool and wore female garments to please her, while she
dressed in the lion skin he was accustomed to wear. A lubricious version of
the story is related by Ovid in *Fa.* (ii, 305ff.).

14. *distaff*] cleft stick around which wool or flax was wound for spinning
by hand.

16–17. *And with this . . . Iphis*] A man of low birth, Iphis fell in love with
the high-born Anaxarete and hung himself when she rejected his suit. (See
Ovid, *Met.*, bk xiv, 802–75 / LCL 698–760.)

22–3. *This fan . . . jealousy*] As noted above (see 1.2.66n.) the turtle dove
was thought to pair for life, and is thus emblematic of constancy (i.e. 'truth'
in love). The jealousy here associated with swans may derive from their fierce
defence of their mates.

23–5. *jealousy . . . folly*] The inextricability of the relationship between
love and jealousy is a recurrent motif in early modern literature (see Tilley,
L510). Compare *England*: 'Surius gave Euphues thanks, allowing [i.e.
approving] his judgement in the description of love, especially in this, that
he would have a woman if she were faithful to be also jealous, which is as
necessary to be required in them as constancy' (p. 315).

24. *dotage*] infatuation.

30. *all . . . rainbow*] Compare Niobe's garland, which changes colour with
the time of day (1.2.5–6).

Cupid. I accept your offers, not without cause; and wonder
at your loves, not without pleasure. But be your thoughts
as true as your words?

Ramis. Thou, Cupid, that givest the wound, knowest the   35
heart; for as impossible it is to conceal our affections as
to resist thy force.

Cupid. I know that where mine arrow lighteth, there breedeth
love; but shooting every minute a thousand shafts, I know
not on whose heart they light – though they fall on no   40
place but hearts. What are your mistresses?

Ramis. Ceres' maidens. Mine most cruel, which she calleth
constancy.

Montanus. Mine most fair, but most proud.

Silvestris. Mine most witty, but most wavering.   45

Cupid. Is the one cruel, th'other coy, the third inconstant?

Ramis. Too cruel!

Montanus. Too coy!

Silvestris. Too fickle!

Cupid. What do they think of Cupid?   50

Ramis. One sayeth he hath no eyes, because he hits he knows
not whom.

Montanus. Th'other that he hath no ears, to hear those that
call.

Silvestris. The third that he hath no nose, for savours are not   55
found of lovers.

---

37. *force*] power.
38. *lighteth*] alights.
46. *coy*] unresponsive, aloof.
55–6. *for savours . . . lovers*] obscure. Bond (iii, p. 567) takes the comment
to mean that lovers do not notice unpleasant smells, citing Shakespeare, *Son.*
130, line 8. The force of the Shakespearian passage, however, is that the
lover is acutely aware of the difference between the smell of perfumes and
the 'reek' which emanates from his mistress's mouth, whom he none the less
loves despite her bad breath. The force of 'found of', moreover, is not
'noticed', or 'detected by', but 'characteristic of'. The comment may thus
allude not to obliviousness to unpleasant odours but to the conventional
neglect of personal hygiene by unrequited lovers (cf. the attribution of
Hamlet's disordered attire and 'stockings foul'd' to love: *Ham.*, 2.1.79), or
the bad breath and susceptibility to wind associated with melancholy (see
Alan Brissenden, ed., *As You Like It*, World's Classics (Oxford, 1993), p. 34).

Ramis. All that he hath no taste, because sweet and sour is
all one.

Montanus. All that he hath no sense, because pains are pleasures and pleasures pains.   60

Silvestris. All that he is a foolish god, working without reason,
and suffering the repulse without regard.

Cupid. Dare they blaspheme my godhead, which Jove doth
worship, Neptune reverence, and all the gods tremble at?
To make them love were a revenge too gentle for Cupid;   65
to make you hate, a recompense too small for lovers. But
of that anon. What have you used in love?

Ramis. All things that may procure love: gifts, words, oaths,
sighs, and swoonings.

Cupid. What said they of gifts?   70

Montanus. That affection could not be bought with gold.

Cupid. What of words?

Ramis. That they were golden blasts out of leaden bellows.

Cupid. What of oaths?

Silvestris. That Jupiter never sware true to Juno.   75

Cupid. What of sighs?

Silvestris. That deceit kept a forge in the hearts of fools.

Cupid. What of swoonings?

Montanus. Nothing, but that they wished them deaths.

Cupid. What reasons gave they not to love?   80

Silvestris. Women's reasons. They would not, because they
would not.

57, 59, 61. *All that*] All say that.

57–8. *sweet . . . one*] lovers embrace both joy and suffering. The assertion
plays upon the proverbial expression, 'Take (mingle) the sweet with the sour'
(Tilley, S1038).

59. *sense*] ability to feel.

59–60. *pains . . . pains*] See 2.1.80–2 and note.

62. *suffering . . . regard*] indifferent to rejection.

63–4. *which Jove doth worship*] to which even the king of the gods must
bow.

73. *golden . . . bellows*] the seemingly beautiful but insubstantial products
of something essentially debased.

77.] The image depends upon the use of bellows to heighten the heat of
a forge. The exhalations of the lover are seen as similarly artificially induced
blasts of air, produced by those foolish enough to engage in amatory
matters.

79. *wished them deaths*] wished that they were deaths.

81–2.] proverbial (Tilley, B179).

Cupid. Well, then shall you see Cupid requite their reasons
  with his rigour. What punishment do you desire that
  Cupid will deny?   85
Ramis. Mine, being so hard as stone, would I have turned to
  stone; that being to lovers pitiless, she may to all the
  world be senseless.
Montanus. Mine, being so fair and so proud, would I have
  turned into some flower, that she may know beauty is as 90
  fading as grass, which, being fresh in the morning, is
  withered before night.
Silvestris. Mine, divine Cupid, whose affection nothing can
  make stayed, let her be turned to that bird that liveth only
  by air, and dieth if she touch the earth, because it is 95
  constant: the bird of paradise, Cupid, that drawing in her
  bowels nothing but air, she may know her heart fed on
  nothing but fickleness.
Cupid. Your revenges are reasonable, and shall be granted.
  Thou, Nisa, whose heart no tears could pierce, shalt with 100
  continual waves be wasted. Instead of thy fair hair, shalt
  thou have green moss; thy face of flint, because thy heart
  is of marble; thine ears shall be holes for fishes, whose
  ears were more deaf than fishes'. Thou, Celia, whom
  beauty made proud, shalt have the fruit of beauty, that 105

---

104. fishes'] *Edge;* fishes *Q.*

83–4. *requite . . . rigour*] repay . . . harshness.

85. *will deny*] elliptical ('will not deny'), i.e. there is no punishment that
Cupid will not grant.

86, 89, 93. *Mine*] My mistress.

87–8. *pitiless . . . senseless*] without pity . . . . without feeling.

90–2. *beauty . . . night*] Compare *Midas*: 'beauty in a minute is both a
blossom and a blast [withered flower]' (2.1.122–3). The transience of female
beauty is proverbial (cf. Tilley, B165 and B169).

94. *stayed*] constant.

94–6. *that bird . . . paradise*] Bond notes that the belief that the newly dis-
covered bird of paradise lived only in the air and fed exclusively on air was
probably attributable to the fact that the skins sold to mariners by the people
of New Guinea were prepared after the legs had been cut off (iii, p. 567).

101. *wasted*] worn away.

103–4. *thine ears . . . deaf than fishes'*] Edge notes, 'fish lack external ears
and so were thought to be deaf' (p. 650).

105–9. *the fruit . . . stalk*] For the transience of female beauty see lines
90–2 and n. above.

105. *fruit*] product, reward.

is, to fade whiles it is flourishing and to blast before it is
blown. Thy face, as fair as the damask rose, shall perish
like the damask rose; the canker shall eat thee in the bud,
and every little wind blow thee from the stalk. And then
shall men in the morning wear thee in their hats, and at   110
night cast thee at their heels. Thou, Niobe, whom nothing
can please (but that which most displeaseth Cupid,
inconstancy), shalt only breathe and suck air for food,
and wear feathers for silk, being more wavering than air,
and lighter than feathers. This will Cupid do. Therefore,   115
when next you shall behold your ladies, do but send a
faithful sigh to Cupid, and there shall arise a thick mist,
which Proserpine shall send. And in the moment you
shall be revenged, and they changed; Cupid prove himself
a great god, and they peevish girls.   120
Ramis. With what sacrifice shall we show ourselves thankful;
or how may we requite this benefit?
Cupid. You shall yearly at my temple offer true hearts, and
hourly bestow all your wits in loving devices. Think all

106–7. *to blast . . . . blown*] to be blighted before it comes to full flower.
See lines 90–2n. above for similar use of the image.

108. *damask rose*] Described in 1578 as 'neither redde nor white, but of
a mixt colour betwixt red and white' (Lyte, *Dodoens*, vi.i, 654: *OED* sb. I 2),
the damask rose is frequently used during the Renaissance as an analogy for
the perfect colouring of the female face. Compare *AYL*: 'There was a pretty
redness in his lip, / A little riper and more lusty red / Than that mix'd in his
cheek; 'twas just the difference / Betwixt the constant red and mingled
damask' (3.5.120–3).

109–11. *And then . . . heels*] See 1.2.15n.

117–19. *there shall arise . . . they changed*] Bond notes that the 'thick mist'
rising from the underworld (see line 118n. below) in which the nymphs are
transformed into subhuman forms parallels the 'shower' (5.4.39) sent from
above by Venus in which they are returned to their human shapes (iii, 567).
The fact that the first transformation is not enacted points, in his view, to
the excision of a scene, but the dramatist may well have elected to leave the
first metamorphosis to the imagination of the audience in order to heighten
the wonder of the second (cf. the off-stage arborification of Bagoa in *Endymion*, and her on-stage return to human form in the final scene).

118. *Proserpine*] Queen of the underworld (from which mists were thought
to arise).

in the moment] at that moment.

119. *prove*] will prove.

120. *peevish*] foolish.

124. *loving devices*] contrivances expressive of love.

the time lost that is not spent in love. Let your oaths be   125
without number, but not without truth; your words full
of alluring sweetness, but not of broad flattery; your
attires neat, but not womanish; your gifts of more price
for the fine device than the great value, and yet of such
value that the device seem not beggarly, nor yourselves   130
blockish. Be secret, that worketh miracles; be constant,
that bringeth secrecy. This is all Cupid doth command.
Away!

Ramis. And to this we all willingly consent.   [*Exit* CUPID.]

Silvestris. Now what resteth but revenge on them that have   135
practised malice on us? Let mine be anything, seeing she
will not be only mine.

Montanus. Let us not now stand wishing, but presently seek
them out, using as great speed in following revenge as we
did in pursuing our love. Certainly we shall find them   140
about Ceres' tree, singing or sacrificing.

134. SD] *This ed.; The temple-doors close. / Bond; Exit. / Daniel (following line
133 this ed.).*   135. SP] *Edge; omitted in Q. Lines 135–7 printed in all other eds
as a continuation of Ramis' preceding speech.*

─────────────────────────────

125–31. *Let your oaths . . . blockish*] The advice carries echoes of that
offered to Phao by the aged Sybilla in *Sappho and Phao* (2.4.61ff.), which in
turn looks back to that of Psellus to Philautus in *England* (p. 261).

127. *broad*] open, gross.

128–31. *your gifts . . . blockish*] Edge notes that the injunction derives from
Ovid (*Ars am.*, ii, 261–2), and refers to '*sigilla* . . . the finely designed trivial
gifts exchanges by lovers' (p. 651).

129–30. *fine device . . . device*] intricacy of the conception . . . contrivance.

131. *blockish*] stupid.

131–2. *Be secret . . . secrecy*] See 2.1.121n.

135–7. *Now what . . . mine*] The lines appear to be assigned to Ramis in
Q and are given to him by all previous editors other than Edge. The layout
of *Q* suggests, however, that the speech by Ramis beginning 'And to all this'
(line 134, this ed.) ended with the word 'consent' in the copy-text, and that
the compositor simply omitted the speech prefix from the start of the ensuing
speech (line 135, this ed.). The content of the passage supports the case for
a change of speaker. It is Niobe (Silvestris' love), not Nisa (beloved of
Ramis) who is inconstant.

135. *resteth*] remains.

138. *presently*] immediately.

140–1. *we shall find . . . sacrificing*] Bond comments: 'since, however, the
rock, rose, and bird to which they are transformed are obviously present in
the last scene . . . which is laid before Cupid's Temple, we have to suppose
the transformation as taking place near the latter, on some visit of the

Silvestris. But shall we not go visit Erisichthon?

Montanus. Not I, lest he eat us, that devoureth all things. His
looks are of force to famish! Let us in, and let all ladies
beware to offend those in spite that love them in honour.   145
For when the crow shall set his foot in their eye, and the
black ox tread on their foot, they shall find their misfortunes to be equal with their deformities, and men both
to loathe and laugh at them.   *Exeunt.*

Actus quartus, Scena secunda

[*Enter*] ERISICHTHON [*and*] PROTEA.

Erisichthon. Come, Protea, tell me, how didst thou escape
from the Merchant?

4.2.0. Actus . . . secunda] *Fairholt (subst.);* ACTVS QUARTVS. SCENA PRIMA
Q; SCENA SECVNDA *Bond;* [IV,ii.] *Edge;* SCENE 2 *Daniel. Bond supplies*
<*Seashore near* ERISICHTHON'S *Farm.*>. 0.1. SD] *Edge (subst.); Erisic-*
thon, Protea, Petulius, Syren. / *Q;* ERISICTHON, PROTEA, PETULIUS, Syren.
<*Enter* ERISICHTHON *and* PROTEA.> / *Bond.*

---

nymphs to the shrine' (p. 567). The observation by Montanus may afford
an indication, however, of the way that the play was initially staged, in that
whereas, in terms of the action, the nymphs' return to human form is effected
near Cupid's temple, the rock, rose, and bird may have been physically
positioned on the part of the stage formerly occupied by Ceres' tree, sustain-
ing the tripart division of the playing space into stances towards love. (See
Introduction, pp. 35–6 above.)

144. *are of force to*] have the power to.
in] go in.

146–7. *when the crow . . . foot*] both images of the aging process, used
elsewhere in the Lylian corpus in relation to love. Compare, 'When the black
crow's foot shall appear in their eye, or the black ox tread on their foot, when
their beauty shall be like the blasted rose . . . who will like of them in their
age who loved none in their youth?' (*Anatomy*, pp. 49–50), and, 'Venus
waxeth old . . . now crow's foot is on her eye, and the black ox hath trod on
her foot' (*Sappho and Phao*, 4.2.21–4). Tilley records both images as proverbial (C865 and O103, 'The black Ox never trod on his foot'), citing,
in relation to the second, A. Taylor, 'The Proverb "The Black Ox Has
Not Trod on His Foot" in Renaissance Literature', *Philological Quarterly* XX
(July 1941), 266–78.

4.2.0. *Actus quartus, Scena secunda*] See Introduction, pp. 1–3, for a discussion of the erroneous headings (see collation note) of this and two later
scenes in *Q.*

1–2.] See 3.2.1n.

Protea. Neptune, that great god, when I was ready to go with
    the Merchant into the ship, turned me to a fisherman on
    the shore, with an angle in my hand, and on my shoulder   5
    a net. The Merchant, missing me and yet finding me,
    asked me who I was, and whether I saw not a fair maiden.
    I answered, 'No!' He, marvelling and raging, was forced
    either to lose his passage or seek for me among the
    pebbles. To make short, a good wind caused him to go   10
    I know not whither, and me (thanks be to Neptune!) to
    return home.

Erisichthon. Thou art happy, Protea, though thy father be
    miserable; and Neptune gracious, though Ceres cruel.
    Thy escape from the Merchant breedeth in me life, joy,   15
    and fullness.

Protea. My father cannot be miserable if Protea be happy; for
    by selling me every day he shall never want meat, nor I
    shifts to escape. And now, father, give me leave to enjoy
    my Petulius, that on this unfortunate shore still seeks me,   20
    sorrowing.

Erisichthon. Seek him, dear Protea. Find and enjoy him; and
    live ever hereafter to thine own comforts, that hast hith-
    erto been the preserver of mine!   *Exit.*

---

10. pebbles.] *Q (Pebbles?).*

  5. *angle*] fishing rod.

  8. *I answered, 'No!'*] Edge comments, 'Protea's emphatic "no!" is humor-
ous – the Merchant asks if she has seen a young lady, and Protea answers
that she has not seen a fair virgin. The quibble on "maiden" is not in Ovid'
(p. 652). The response, however, is more likely to be a simple statement of
fact, in that Protea cannot have seen herself in the sense that the Merchant
intends.

   marvelling] wondering, in a state of amazement.

  9. *lose his passage*] miss his opportunity to put to sea.

  13. *happy*] fortunate.

  18–19. *want meat . . . shifts*] lack food . . . expedients.

  19. *enjoy*] be joined in love with.

  20. *unfortunate*] Bond suggests (iii, p. 568) that the shore is 'unfortunate'
because it is 'rocky', citing 4.2.87 (this ed.). The presence of a single rock
is insufficient, however, to suggest the dangerousness of the coast, and it is
possible that Protea's use of the adjective merely refers to the anxiety and
sorrow that she and Petulius have endured there.

  22–4.] Erisichthon's release of Protea from her filial obligations appears
to run counter to the latter's assertion that he can now preserve his life by

[The] SIREN *[is disclosed, sitting on a rock]*.

Protea. Ay me, behold, a Siren haunts this shore. The gods   25
    forbid she should entangle my Petulius!

Siren. *[To herself]* Accursed men, whose loves have no other
    mean than extremities, nor hates' end but mischief!

Protea. *[Aside]* Unnatural monster! No maid, that accuseth
    men, whose loves are built on truth and whose hearts are   30
    removed by courtesy. I will hear the depth of her malice.
                                                  [She stands aside.]

Siren. Of all creatures most unkind, most cunning; by whose
    subtleties I am half fish, half flesh, themselves being
    neither fish nor flesh. In love luke-warm, in cruelty red
    hot. If they praise, they flatter; if flatter, deceive; if   35
    deceive, destroy.

24.1. SD] *This ed.; Syren.* / *Q (following line 26 this ed.); Syren appears.* /
Fairholt, Edge (positioning as Q); Enter Siren. / *Daniel (positioning as this
ed.).* 27. SD] *This ed.* 28. hates'] *This ed.;* hates *Q.* 29. SD] *Edge.*
30. loves . . . whose] *Q; not in Fairholt.* 31.1. SD] *This ed.*

selling her every day (lines 17–18). Since she goes on in the same speech to
ask for his consent to her union with Petulius, however, Protea herself does
not appear to view her two roles as incompatible. Edge suggests that 'probably Lyly wanted to show Erisichthon moved by love, and a permanent
release from hunger is not intended' (p. 652).

   25. *Ay me*] an exclamation of dismay or distress.

   Siren] See p. 53, line 15n.

   27–8. *have no other . . . extremeties*] (*a*) know no kind of moderation
between extremes of behaviour; (*b*) have no other method of advancement
than through extravagant conduct. The assertion constitutes a reversal of
the proverb 'A woman either loves or hates to extremes' (Tilley, W651),
which attributes extremes of behaviour to women rather than men. Compare
Endymion: 'He shall know the malice of a woman to have neither mean nor
end' (1.2.57–8).

   28. *nor hates' end but mischief*] nor their hatred any other outcome than
injurious deeds.

   31. *removed*] moved, affected (*OED* v.I 8b).

   32–3. *by whose subtleties . . . flesh*] As Bond notes (iii, p. 568), 'a previous
deception by man forms no part of the classical myth of the Sirens, who
were made like birds and condemned to their alluring part by Ceres for not
assisting Proserpine (Hyg, *Fab.* 141)'.

   34. *neither . . . flesh*] proverbial (Tilley, F319), used to express an
indeterminate or fluctuating state of mind or condition. The Siren claims
that she has become literally ambivalent as a product of the ambiguity of
men.

Protea. [*Aside*] She rails at men, but seeks to entangle them.
This sleight is prepared for my sweet Petulius. I will
withdraw myself close, for Petulius followeth. He will,
without doubt, be enamoured of her; enchanted he shall   40
not be. My charms shall countervail hers. It is he hath
saved my father's life with money, and must prolong
mine with love.   [*She conceals herself.*]

[*Enter* PETULIUS.]

Petulius. I marvel Protea is so far before me. If she run, I'll
fly. [*Calling*] Sweet Protea, where art thou? It is Petulius   45
calleth Protea!
Siren. [*Aside*] Here cometh a brave youth! Now, Siren, leave
out nothing that may allure: thy golden locks, thy enticing looks, thy tuned voice, thy subtle speech, thy fair
promises, which never missed the heart of any but   50
Ulysses.

Sing, with a glass in her hand, and a comb.

---

37. SD] *This ed.*   43. SD] *This ed.; Withdraws / Edge.*   43.1. SD] *Bond.*
45. SD] *This ed.*   47. SD] *This ed.*   51.1. SD. *Sing*] *Q; Sings / Fairholt;*
She sings / Daniel.

---

37. *rails at*] verbally abuses.
38. *sleight*] trick (here the Siren's deceptive allure).
39. *withdraw myself close*] retire and conceal myself.
41. *countervail*] counterbalance.
41-2. *It is he . . . money*] The revelation that Petulius has helped to
feed Erisichthon supplies both a naturalistic explanation for the latter's
survival once his own means are exhausted and an index of the former's
fitness to partner Protea, in that he is similarly activated by generosity of
spirit.
44. *marvel*] am surprised.
46. *calleth*] who calls.
47. *brave*] handsome.
50-1. *which never . . . Ulysses*] Ulysses resisted the alluring songs of the
Siren by tying himself to the mast of his own ship and stopping the ears of
his sailors with wax (*Odyssey*, bk xii).
51.1. *Sing*] The imperative form is retained here (see collation note), and
at 56.1 below, in that the direction may be an authorial injunction rather
than a description of stage business, given Lyly's close involvement in the
production of his plays.
    with a glass . . . comb] See p. 53, line 15n.
    glass] mirror.

Petulius. What divine goddess is this? What sweet harmony?
My heart is ravished with such tickling thoughts, and
mine eyes stayed with such a bewitching beauty that I
can neither find the means to remove my affection nor   55
to turn aside my looks.
                                        Sing again Siren.
I yield to death, but with such delight that I would not
wish to live, unless it were to hear thy sweet lays.
Siren. Live still, so thou love me. [*He stares at her.*] Why
standest thou amazed at the word 'love'?   60
Protea. [*From her place of hiding*] It is high time to prevent this
mischief! Now, Neptune, stand to thy promise, and let
me take suddenly the shape of an old man. So shall I mar
what she makes.   [*She disappears from view.*]
Petulius. [*To the Siren*] Not yet come to myself, or if I be, I   65
dare not credit mine ears. Love thee, divine goddess?
Vouchsafe I may honour thee, and live by the imagination I have of thy words and worthiness.

56.1. SD] *Q (Sing againe Syren.); She sings again. / Daniel.* 59. SD] *This
ed.* 61. SD] *This ed.; behind / Bond; from behind / Edge.* 64. SD] *This ed.;
Exit into the structure at back. / Bond; Exit. / Edge.* 65. SD] *This ed.*
66. mine] *Q;* my *Fairholt.*

53. *tickling*] pleasurable (here with sexual overtones).
54. *stayed*] arrested.
55. *remove my affection*] shake off the attraction I feel.
56.1. *Sing again*] See 4.2.51.1n.
58. *lays*] songs.
62. *stand to thy promise*] keep your word.
63. *take suddenly*] assume without delay.
63–4. *So shall . . . makes*] a variation on the common formulation 'to
make or mar' (Tilley, M48), i.e. to bring something to fruition or utterly
destroy it.
64. SD] The stage direction interpolated by Bond here ('*Exit into the
structure at back*') imposes a mode of staging upon the play for which no
contemporary evidence exists. For a similar example of his introduction of
unwarranted directions see his repeated references to a trap in 3.2. of *The
Woman in the Moon.*
65. *Not yet . . . myself*] an elliptical response to the Siren's question at
lines 59–60. Petulius has not yet come sufficiently to himself (i.e. is still too
rapt by the initial impression created by the Siren and astonished by her
offer of love) to be able to formulate a reply.
67. *Vouchsafe I may*] Deign to allow me to.
67–8. *the imagination I have*] my fancied understanding.

Siren. I am a goddess, but a lady and a virgin, whose love, if
    thou embrace, thou shalt live no less happy than the gods   70
    in heaven.

             [Protea appears in the shape of an old man.]

Protea. Believe not this enchantress, sweet youth, who
    retaineth the face of a virgin but the heart of a fiend;
    whose sweet tongue sheddeth more drops of blood than
    it uttereth syllables.   75

Petulius. Out, dotterel, whose dim eyes cannot discern beauty,
    nor doting age judge of love!

Protea. If thou listen to her words, thou shalt not live to
    repent, for her malice is as sudden as her joys are
    sweet.   80

Petulius. Thy silver hairs are not so precious as her golden
    locks, nor thy crooked age of that estimation as her flow-
    ering youth.

Siren. [*To Petulius*] That old man measureth the hot assault
    of love with the cold skirmishes of age.   85

---

69. I . . . goddess] *Q;* I am <not> a goddesse *Bond;* I am not a goddess
Edge. 71.1. SD] *This ed.; Re-enter* PROTEA *as an old man.* / *Bond.*
84. SD] *This ed.*

---

69. *I am a goddess*] All previous editors, with the exception of Fairholt,
assume that the word 'not' has been omitted here and thus that the Siren is
repudiating the divinity Petulius ascribes to her. It is equally possible,
however, that the Siren is conceding her (supposed) godhead, but indicating
that she is nevertheless a nubile young woman ('a lady and a virgin'). Relationships between mortals and deities occur frequently in classical myth, and
the Siren may merely be indicating that her divinity does not make her
unavailable to a human lover.

76. *dotterel*] a species of plover noted for the ease with which it could be
caught, and hence used to denote a fool. As Bond notes (iii, p. 568), the
term is a derivative of 'dote' (cf. dotard).

76, 81. *dim eyes . . . silver hairs*] evidences of Protea's transformation into
an old man.

79. *sudden*] swift (with connotations of violence).

84–5.] Compare Euphues' response to the advice of the aged Eubulus in
Anatomy: 'Do you measure the hot assaults of youth by the cold skirmishes
of age?' (p. 40).

84, 86. *That old man . . . That young cruel*] Protea in her translated
form . . . The Siren.

Protea. That young cruel resembleth old apes, who kill by
culling. From the top of this rock, whereon she sitteth,
will she throw thee headlong into the sea, whose song is
the instrument of her witchcraft. Never smiling but when
she meaneth to smite, and under the flattery of love   90
practiseth the shedding of blood.

Petulius. What art thou, which so blasphemest this divine
creature?

Protea. I am the ghost of Ulysses, who continually hover
about these places where this Siren haunteth, to save   95
those which otherwise should be spoiled. Stop thine ears,
as I did mine, and succour the fair – but by thy folly the
most infortunate – Protea.

Petulius. Protea? What dost thou hear, Petulius? Where is
Protea?   100

Protea. In this thicket, ready to hang herself, because thou
carest not for her that did swear to follow. Curse this hag,
who only hath the voice and face of a virgin, the rest all
fish, and feathers, and filth. Follow me, and strongly stop
thine ears, lest the second encounter make the wound   105
incurable.

Petulius. Is this a Siren, and thou Ulysses? Cursed be that
hellish carcass, and blessed be thy heavenly spirit!

---

98. infortunate] *Q;* unfortunate *Daniel.*   102. did] *Q;* did<st> *Bond.*

86–7. *old apes . . . culling*] Compare Lyly's defence of his publication of
the two parts of *Euphues*: 'Glad I was to send them both abroad lest, making
a wanton of my first with a blind conceit, I should resemble the ape and kill
it by culling it' (p. 157). The image is proverbial and denotes the destructive-
ness of immoderate affection (cf. Tilley, A264: 'The Ape kills her young with
kindness (by clipping)'.

87. *culling*] embracing (from Fr. *accoler*).

91. *practiseth*] engages in.

94. *I am . . . Ulysses*] As Edge points out, the classical myths invoked here
are incompatible in that Ulysses was the grandson of Autolycus, who married
the daughter of Erisichthon (p. 654). For a similar conflation of disparate
periods and persons in the Lylian corpus see the assemblage of philosophers
at the court of Alexander in *Campaspe.*

96. *spoiled*] destroyed.

98. *infortunate*] unfortunate.

104. *feathers*] See p. 53, line 15n.

Siren. I shrink my head for shame. Oh, Ulysses, is it not
    enough for thee to escape, but also to teach others? Sing   110
    and die! Nay, die and never sing more.
                             [*The* SIREN *disappears.*]
Protea. Follow me at this door, and out at the other.
                [*Exeunt. They re-enter by another door,*
                     PROTEA *in her own shape.*]
Petulius. How am I delivered! The old man is vanished, and
    here for him stands Protea!
Protea. Here standeth Protea, that hath saved thy life. Thou   115
    must also prolong hers. But let us into the woods, and
    there I will tell thee how I came to Ulysses, and the sum
    of all my fortunes, which happily will breed in thee both
    love and wonder.
Petulius. I will, and only love Protea, and never cease to   120
    wonder at Protea!
                                   Exeunt.

111.1. SD] *This ed.; Exit. / Edge.*   112.1–2. SD] *This ed.; They pass through
the central structure,* PROTEA *emerging in her own character. / Bond; Exit. Enter*
Protea *at another door, appearing as herself. / Edge.*   118. happily] *Q;* haply
Daniel.

---

109. *shrink*] draw in.
111.1.] See Introduction, p. 38n. 114 for a discussion of how this spectacle
may have been effected.
112.] As previous commentators have noted, Protea is referring here not
to the dramatic environment but to the theatrical arena in which the action
takes place. Chambers suggests that the doors may be those of Erisichthon's
house, but notes that 'they do not prove that a *domus* of Erisichthon was
visible; they may be merely stage-doors' (iii, p. 34n.). For an alternative
explanation of the implied directions see Introduction, note 105.
112.1. They re-enter . . . door] The stage direction is derived from Protea's injunction in the previous line to 'Follow me at this door, and out at
the other'. Bond's '*They pass through the central structure*' is without textual
justification and again imposes a staging on the play for which no contemporary evidence exists (cf. line 64 SD.n.).
113. *delivered*] saved, rescued from danger.
115–16. *Thou must . . . hers*] Compare lines 41–3: 'he hath saved my
father's life with money, and must prolong mine with love'.
117. *came to*] came to be.
118. *happily will*] will perhaps.

Act 5

Actus quintus, Scena prima

[*Enter*] CERES, CUPID, [*and*] TIRTENA.

Ceres. Cupid, thou hast transformed my nymphs, and
incensed me; them to shapes unreasonable, me to anger
immortal. For at one time I am both robbed of mine
honour and my nymphs.

Cupid. Ceres, thy nymphs were stubborn, and thyself, speak-   5
ing so imperiously to Cupid, somewhat stately. If you ask
the cause in choler, *sic volo, sic iubeo*; if in courtesy, *quae
venit ex merito poena dolenda venit.* They were disdainful,
and have their deserts. Thou, Ceres, dost but govern the
guts of men; I the hearts. Thou seekest to starve Erisich-   10
thon with thy minister, Famine, whom his daughter shall
preserve by my virtue, love.

5.1.0. Actus . . . prima] *Q*; [V,i.] *Edge*; Act 5 SCENE I *Daniel. Bond supplies*
<*Before the Temple of* CUPID.>. 0.1. SD] *Q (subst.); [Enter]* Ceres, Cupid,
Tirtena [*attending* Ceres]. / *Edge.* 8. *poena] Q;* paena *Edge.* 11. minister,
Famine] *Bond (*famine*);* ministred famine *Q;* minister'd famine *Edge;* min-
istered famine *Daniel.*

5.1.2. *unreasonable*] senseless, devoid of reason. Compare *R&J*: 'thy wild
acts denote / The unreasonable fury of a beast' (3.3.110–11).

3. *immortal*] undying.

6. *stately*] haughty, arrogant (*OED* adj. 2a).

7. *choler*] anger.

sic volo, sic iubeo] A variant of Juvenal's *hoc volo, sic iubeo* ('it's my wish
and my command': *Satires*, vi, 223), Cupid's response constitutes an assertion
of absolute power. The words derive from Juvenal's description of a domineering woman who crucifies a slave simply because she wishes to do so.

7–8. quae venit . . . venit] a punishment which comes deservedly comes
painfully. The comment is adapted from Ovid's 'Quae venit indigno poena,
dolenda venit' ('The penalty that comes without deserving brings us dole':
Her., v. 8).

11. *minister, Famine*] Though *Q*'s 'ministred famine' is preserved in the
majority of editions (see collation note), Bond's emendation is adopted here
because it avoids the awkwardness of an unusual (and highly unlikely) construction, and heightens the balance between the instruments of the two
deities – starvation and love.

Ceres. Thou art but a god, Cupid.

Cupid. No, Ceres, but such a god as maketh thunder fall out
of Jove's hand by throwing thoughts into his heart, and   15
to be more terrified with the sparkling of a lady's eye than
men with the flashes of his lightning; such a god that hath
kindled more fire in Neptune's bosom than the whole sea
which he is king of can quench. Such power have I that
Pluto's never-dying fire doth but scorch in respect of my   20
flames. Diana hath felt some motions of love; Vesta doth;
Ceres shall.

Ceres. Art thou so cruel?

Cupid. To those that resist, a lion; to those that submit, a
lamb.   25

Ceres. Canst thou make such difference in affection, and yet
shall it all be love?

Cupid. Yea, as much as between sickness and health, though
in both be life. Those that yield, and honour Cupid, shall
possess sweet thoughts, and enjoy pleasing wishes; the   30
other shall be tormented with vain imaginations and
impossible hopes.

14. as] *Q;* that *Fairholt, Bond.*

---

13. *but a god*] only a god, i.e. not superior to Ceres herself.

16. *sparkling . . . eye*] fire flashing from a woman's glance. Compare *LLL*:
'women's eyes . . . / . . . sparkle still the right Promethean fire' (4.3.324–5).
See also 'Let us endure the bending of their fair brows, and the scorching
of their sparkling eyes' at 5.3.8–9 below.

17. *his*] Jove's.

20. *Pluto's never-dying fire*] the undying flames of the god of the
underworld.

in respect of] in comparison to.

21. *Diana . . . love*] The claim looks back to the emotions stirred by
Cupid in Diana's nymphs in *Galatea*, strengthening the case for a close
relationship between the two plays.

Vesta] Roman goddess of the hearth, attended by virgin priestesses and
as pure as the flame by which she was represented. The reference to her
having felt the influence of Cupid may look back to a riddling exchange in
Endymion, initiated, like Cupid's response here, by the formulation 'but a'.
Compare: *Tellus.* Why, she [Cynthia] is but a woman. / *Endymion.* No more
was Venus. / *Tellus.* She is but a virgin. / *Endymion.* No more was Vesta'
(*Endymion*, 2.1.89–92).

26. *affection*] passion.

28–9. *as much . . . life*] i.e. passion encompasses a range of positive and
negative states, just as living embraces a broad spectrum of physical
conditions.

Ceres. How may my nymphs be restored?

Cupid. If thou restore Erisichthon, they embrace their loves,
and all offer sacrifice to me.   35

Ceres. Erisichthon did in contempt hew down my sacred
tree.

Cupid. Thy nymphs did in disdain scorn my constant love.

Ceres. He slew, most cruelly, my chaste Fidelia, whose blood
lieth yet on the ground.   40

Cupid. But Diana hath changed her blood to fresh flowers,
which are to be seen on the ground.

Ceres. What honour shall he do to Ceres? What amends can
he make to Fidelia?

Cupid. All Ceres' grove shall he deck with garlands, and   45
account every tree holy. A stately monument shall
he erect in remembrance of Fidelia, and offer yearly
sacrifice.

Ceres. What sacrifice shall I and my nymphs offer thee? For
I will do anything to restore my nymphs, and honour   50
thee.

Cupid. You shall present, in honour of my mother Venus,
grapes and wheat, for *sine Cerere et Baccho friget Venus.*
You shall suffer your nymphs to play, sometimes to be
idle, in the favour of Cupid; for *otia si tollas, periere Cupi-*   55
dinis arcus. So much for Ceres. Thy nymphs shall make
no vows to continue virgins, nor use words to disgrace
love, nor fly from opportunities that kindle affections. If
they be chaste, let them not be cruel; if fair, not proud;
if loving, not inconstant. Cruelty is for tigers, pride for   60
peacocks, inconstancy for fools.

---

53. sine . . . Venus] without Ceres [i.e. bread] and Bacchus [i.e. wine],
Venus [i.e. love] grows cold. Tilley cites numerous examples of the proverb
including three from Lyly's work (C211).

54. *suffer*] permit.

55. *in the favour of Cupid*] for Cupid's benefit. The injunction, like those
that follow, looks back to Cupid's exchange with Ceres at 2.1.107ff.

55–6. otia . . . arcus] take away leisure and Cupid's bow is broken (Ovid,
Rem. am., 139).

60–1. *Cruelty . . . fools*] The association between tigers and cruelty is a
commonplace in Renaissance literature (cf. Bevington, in Hunter and
Bevington, eds, *Galatea: Midas*, 4.2.29–30, LN), as is the link between

Ceres. Cupid, I yield; and they shall. But, sweet Cupid, let
     them not be deceived by flattery, which taketh the shape
     of affection, nor by lust, which is clothed in the habit of
     love; for men have as many sleights to delude as they have   65
     words to speak.
Cupid. Those that practise deceit shall perish. Cupid favo-
     ureth none but the faithful.
Ceres. Well, I will go to Erisichthon, and bring him before
     thee.   70
Cupid. Then shall thy nymphs recover their forms, so as they
     yield to love.
Ceres. They shall.   *Exeunt.*

---

71. forms] *Fairholt (*formes); fames *Q.*

---

peacocks and pride (cf. Tilley, P157). Edge suggests that the equation
between fools and inconstancy involves a play 'on the homonym "fowls" ',
noting that 'certain birds were proverbially foolish (the lapwing, the hobby)
or inconstant (the sparrow, the cuckoo)', and arguing that Cupid is alluding
here to the transformation of Niobe (p. 656).
    63–4. *taketh . . . affection*] disguises itself as love.
    64. *habit*] garment.
    65. *sleights*] tricks.
    71. *forms*] former shapes. Fairholt's emendation is adopted here, in pref-
erence to *Q* 'fames' (see collation note), contrary to the argument advanced
by Edge that the 'Quarto reading makes perfectly good sense' and that
'emendation seems unnecessary' (p. 656). The sense of the word 'fame' in
Campaspe (1.1.66), which he adduces in support of his position, however,
and which is glossed by Hunter as 'reputation for spotless purity' (Hunter
and Bevington, eds, *Campaspe: Sappho and Phao*), has no bearing on the
situation in *Love's Metamorphosis*, which turns on the restoration not of
character or reputation but of physical shape. The emphasis placed by both
Cupid and Ceres in 5.4 on the physical monstrosity to which the nymphs
will be condemned if they continue to resist the will of the gods confirms
that it is not the 'fames' but the ultimate 'forms' of the nymphs that is at
issue.
    so as] provided that.

Actus quintus, Scena secunda

[*Enter*] PETULIUS [*and*] PROTEA.

Petulius. A strange discourse, Protea, by which I find the gods
amorous, and virgins immortal; goddesses full of cruelty,
and men of unhappiness.

Protea. I have told both my father's misfortunes, grown by
stoutness, and mine, by weakness; his thwarting of Ceres,   5
my yielding to Neptune.

Petulius. I know, Protea, that hard iron falling into fire waxeth
soft, and then the tender heart of a virgin, being in love,
must needs melt. For what should a fair, young, and witty

5.2.0. Scena secunda] *Fairholt (subst.);* SCENA PRIMA *Q;* [V,ii.] *Edge;*
SCENE 2 *Daniel. Bond supplies location* <*The same.*>. 2. immortal; goddesses full] *Punctuation this ed.;* immortall goddesses, full *Q;* immortal,
goddesses full *Fairholt.*

5.2.0. *Scena secunda*] See Introduction, pp. 1–3, for a discussion of the
erroneous headings (see collation note) of this and two other scenes in *Q*.
    1. *discourse*] story (i.e. the account of her history promised by Protea to
Petulius at the close of Act 4).
    1–2. *the gods amorous*] The comment refers to Neptune's seduction of
Protea.
    2. *virgins immortal*] Edge glosses 'immortal' as 'inhuman' and suggests
that Petulius is referring to the transformation of Ceres' nymphs into subhuman forms (p. 657), but lines 4–6 indicate that it is her own history that
Protea has related, not that of Nisa, Celia, and Niobe. It is more likely that
'immortal' in this context signifies 'divine' and that Petulius is alluding to
Protea's superhuman capacity to change shape.
    immortal; goddesses full] A more emphatic version of Fairholt's punctuation
(followed by all subsequent editors) is adopted here (see collation note) in
that the pointing in *Q* ('immortal goddesses, full') disrupts both the sense
of the passage and the syntactic patterning at work in the speech as a whole.
The positioning of a comma after 'goddesses' not only destroys the parallel
with 'gods' in the preceding clause but limits Petulius' observation to an
aspect of the play (the intransigence of the nymphs) which is peripheral to
the story that Protea has related (see lines 4–6).
    2–3. *goddesses . . . unhappiness*] Petulius' summary of the relationship
between Ceres and Erisichthon registers a shift in sympathy from the out-
raged goddess to the offending mortal that prepares the audience for the
denouement of the play.
    5. *stoutness*] obduracy.

lady answer to the sweet enticements of love, but *molle*   10
   meum levibus cor est violabile telis?

Protea. I have heard, too, that hearts of men, stiffer than steel,
   have by love been made softer than wool, and then they
   cry, *omnia vincit Amor: et nos cedamus Amori.*

Petulius. Men have often feigned sighs.   15

Protea. And women forged tears.

Petulius. Suppose I love not?

Protea. Suppose I care not?

Petulius. If men swear and lie, how will you try their loves?

Protea. If women swear they love, how will you try their   20
   dissembling?

Petulius. The gods put wit into women.

Protea. And Nature deceit into men.

Petulius. I did this but to try your patience.

Protea. Nor I, but to prove your faith. [*They approach the* 25
   transformed nymphs.] But see, Petulius, what miraculous
   punishments here are for deserts in love. This rock was
   a nymph to Ceres, so was this rose, so that bird.

---

11. *levibus . . . telis*] *Q; lenibus . . . telit | Fairholt; levibus . . . telit | Daniel.*
25–6. SD] *This ed.*

10–11. molle . . . telis] tender is my heart, and easily pierced by the light
shaft. The quotation is from Ovid (*Her.*, xv, 79) and follows William Lily's
Latin grammar in its omission of *que* from *levibusque* (see Andreadis, 4.1.36–
7n.). An adaptation of the same quotation is used in *Mother Bombie*, where
it is translated as 'a woman's heart is thrust through with a feather' (Andreadis
(ed.), 4.1.37–8).

12. *stiffer than steel*] proverbial (Tilley, S839).

14. omnia . . . Amori] love conquers all; let us, too, yield to Love (Virgil,
Eclogues, x, 69).

19, 20. try] make trial of.

24–5. *I did . . . faith*] Bond suggests that 'Petulius is perhaps excusing his
affair with the Syren, while Protea's answer refers to hers with Neptune' (iii,
p. 569). As Edge notes, however, it is more likely that they are referring 'to
the preceding badinage' (p. 657).

25. *Nor I, but to*] And I only to.

27. *deserts*] conduct meriting reward or punishment. Bond notes (iii,
p. 569) that the word signifies 'deserters, defaulters' but offers no evidence
that it was capable of bearing this meaning.

27–8. *This rock . . . bird*] The demonstrative adjectives confirm that the
objects into which the nymphs have been transformed are visible on stage.
Edge suggests that 'the bird is fluttering above the stage on wires' since 'it
was described earlier as living always in air' and that 'Protea's shift from

Petulius. All changed from their shapes?

Protea. All changed by Cupid, because they disdained love,   30
or dissembled in it.

Petulius. A fair warning to Protea. I hope she will love without
dissembling.

Protea. An item for Petulius, that he delude not those that
love him; for Cupid can also change men. Let us in.   35

Exeunt.

Actus quintus, Scena tertia

[*Enter*] RAMIS, MONTANUS, [*and*] SILVESTRIS.

Ramis. This goeth luckily, that Cupid hath promised to
restore our mistresses, and Ceres that they shall accept
our loves.

Montanus. I did ever imagine that true love would end with
sweet joys, though it was begun with deep sighs.   5

Silvestris. But how shall we look on them, when we shall see
them smile? We must, and perchance they will frown.

Ramis. Tush! Let us endure the bending of their fair brows,
and the scorching of their sparkling eyes, so that we may
possess, at last, the depth of their affections.   10

5.3.0. Scena tertia] *Fairholt (subst.); SCENA QVARTA Q; [V,iii.] Edge; SCENE 3 Daniel. Bond supplies location <The same.>.* 7. We must, and ... will frown] *Q;* We must, and . . . will, frowne *Bond.*

"this" to "that" may indicate that the bird is somewhat removed from the other objects' (p. 657). Other means of representing the bird are possible, however, than that which Edge suggests (e.g. a painted board with a bird in flight), while the greater distance implied by the use of 'that' may relate to the position of the speaker relative to the three objects, rather than to that of the bird relative to the rock and the flower.

32. *fair*] clear, plain (*OED* A adj. IV 17).

34. *item*] admonition (*OED* B sb. 1).

5.3.0. *Scena tertia*] See Introduction, pp. 1–3, for a discussion of the erroneous headings (see collation note) of this and two earlier scenes in Q.

7. *We must*] We will be obliged to face them.

perchance] perhaps.

Montanus. Possess? Never doubt it, for Ceres hath restored
Erisichthon, and therefore will persuade with them. Nay,
command them.

Silvestris. If it come by commandment of Ceres, not their own
motions, I rather they should hate. For what joy can there   15
be in our lives, or in our loves sweetness, when every kiss
shall be sealed with a curse, and every kind word proceed
of fear, not affection? Enforcement is worse than
enchantment.

Ramis. Art thou so superstitious in love, that wast wont to be   20
most careless? Let them curse all day, so I may have but
one kiss at night.

Montanus. Thou art worse than Silvestris! He not content
without absolute love, thou with indifferent.

Silvestris. But here cometh Ceres with Erisichthon. Let us   25
look demurely, for in her heart she hates us deeply.

                                        [*They stand aside.*]

---

16. loves] *Q;* love's *Fairholt;* loves' *Edge.*   20. wast] *Q;* was *Fairholt.*
26.1. SD] *This ed.*

15. *motions*] impulses.
16. *or in our loves sweetness*] or sweetness in our loves.
18–19. *Enforcement . . . enchantment*] a portmanteau allusion, as Edge
notes (p. 658), combining *Ars am.*, ii, 687 ('Pleasure given as a duty has no
charms for me') and *Rem. am.*, 259 ('No hearts will lay aside their passion
by enchantment'). The use of both force and witchcraft to gain love are
repudiated elsewhere in Lyly's work. Hephestion, for example, tells Alexander in *Campaspe* that 'Affection cometh not by appointment or birth, and
then as good hated as enforced' (2.2.114–16), while Floscula warns Tellus
in *Endymion* that 'Affection that is bred by enchantment is like a flower that
is wrought in silk: in colour and form most like, but nothing at all in substance or savour' (1.2.76–8).
20. *superstitious*] exacting.
21. *so*] provided that.
24. *indifferent*] apathetic, lacking in interest or feeling.
26. *demurely*] gravely. Compare *MerVen.*: 'If I do not put on a sober
habit, / Talk with respect . . . / Wear prayer-books in my pocket, look
demurely, / . . . / Like one well studied in a sad ostent / To please his
grandam, never trust me more' (2.2.181–8).

Actus quintus, Scena ultima

[*Enter*] ERISICHTHON, [*restored to his former state, and*]
CERES.

Erisichthon. I will hallow thy woods with solemn feasts, and
honour all thy nymphs with due regard.
Ceres. Well, do so. And thank Cupid, that commands. Nay,
thank my foolish nymphs, that know not how to obey.
[*The foresters come forward.*] Here be the lovers, ready at   5
receipt. – How now, gentlemen, what seek you?
Ramis. Nothing, but what Ceres would find.
Ceres. Ceres hath found those that I would she had lost: vain
lovers.
Ramis. Ceres may lose that that Cupid would save: true   10
lovers.
Ceres. You think so, one of another?
Silvestris. Cupid knoweth so of us all.
Ceres. You might have made me a counsel of your loves.

5.4.0. Actus quintus, Scena ultima] *Q (subst.);* [V,iv.] *Edge;* SCENE 4
Daniel. Bond omits Q ACTVS QVINTUS *and supplies location* <*The
same.*>. 0.1–2. SD. [*Enter*] . . . CERES.] *This ed.; Cupid, Ceres, Nymphes,
Erisicthon, Petulius, Protea.* / *Q;* CUPID, CERES, Nymphes, ERISICTHON,
PETULIUS, PROTEA. <*Enter, to the* Foresters, CERES *and* ERISICHTHON.>
/ *Bond; Enter* Ceres, Erisichthon. / *Edge; Enter* ERISICHTHON, CERES, PETU-
LIUS, PROTEA, *and* CUPID, *to* RAMIS, SILVESTRIS, *and* MONTANUS, *who
remain.* / *Daniel.* 5. SD] *This ed.*

5.4.0.1. restored to his former state] See line 16 below and 3.2.0.1n.
1. *hallow*] honour.
2. *regard*] respect.
3–4. *Nay . . . obey*] Erisichthon is indebted to Ceres' nymphs in that it is
their disobedience that has obliged Ceres to agree to the lifting of his
punishment.
5–6. *at receipt*] to intercept us (a hunting term, used for the position
towards which game was driven). Compare *England*: 'I had as lief stand at
the receipt as at the loosing' (p. 311).
7.] The aims of Ceres and the foresters are identical, since both seek the
restoration of the metamorphosed nymphs.
14.] Compare Alexander's response to the discovery of Apelles' love for
Campaspe: 'Methinks I might have been made privy to your affection;
though my counsel had not been necessary, yet my countenance [approval]
might have been thought requisite' (*Campaspe*, 5.4.108–10). The comment
reflects Elizabeth's stance towards amatory relationships between members
of her court.

Montanus. Ay, madam, if love would admit counsel.   15

[*Enter* CUPID *from his temple.*]

Ceres. Cupid, here is Erisichthon in his former state; restore
my nymphs to theirs. Then shall they embrace these
lovers, who wither out their youth.
Erisichthon. Honoured be mighty Cupid, that makes me
live!   20

[*Enter* PETULIUS *and* PROTEA.]

Petulius. Honoured be mighty Cupid, that makes me love!
Protea. And me!
Ceres. What, more lovers yet? I think it be impossible for
Ceres to have any follow her in one hour that is not in
love in the next!   25
Cupid. Erisichthon, be thou careful to honour Ceres, and
forget not to please her nymphs. The faithful love of thy
daughter Protea hath wrought both pity in me to grant
her desires, and to release thy punishments. – Thou,
Petulius, shalt enjoy thy love, because I know thee   30
loyal.
Petulius. Then shall Petulius be most happy.
Protea. And Protea most fortunate.
Cupid. But do you, Ramis, continue your constant love? And
you, Montanus? And you, Silvestris?   35
Ramis. Nothing can alter our affections, which increase
while the means decrease, and wax stronger in being
weakened.

15.1. SD] *This ed.; The temple-doors open.* / *Bond; The temple doors open,
revealing* Cupid. / *Edge.* 20. live] *Q;* love *Fairholt.* 20.1. SD] *Bond
(subst.), following line 18 this ed.* 21. Petulius . . . love] *Not in Fairholt.*

15. *if love . . . counsel*] proverbial. Edge (p. 659) cites Tilley, *Elizabethan
Proverb Lore* (Ann Arbor, 1926), 74: 'Love admits no counsel'.
30–1. *because I know thee loyal*] The comment seems surprising in view of
Petulius' failure to resist the allure of the Siren. The fact that it is the mention
of Protea, however, that leads him to reject the Siren's advance may be seen
as indicative that he is fundamentally 'loyal'.
36–7. *which increase . . . decrease*] which grow as the means of fulfilment
diminish.

Cupid. Then, Venus, send down that shower wherewith thou
    wert wont to wash those that do thee worship, and let   40
    love, by thy beams, be honoured in all the world, and
    feared, wished for, and wondered at.
                         [*A shower falls from above.*]
    Here are thy nymphs, Ceres.
                    [*The nymphs emerge from the shower.*]
Ramis. Whom do I see? Nisa?
Montanus. Divine Celia! Fairer than ever she was!   45
Silvestris. My sweet Niobe!
                    [*The nymphs make no response.*]
Ceres. Why stare you, my nymphs, as amazed? Triumph,
    rather, because you have your shapes. This great god,
    Cupid, that for your prides and follies changed, hath by
    my prayer and promise restored you.   50
Cupid. You see, ladies, what it is to make a mock of love, or
    a scorn of Cupid. See where your lovers stand. You must
    now take them for your husbands. This is my judgement;
    this is Ceres' promise.
Ramis. Happy Ramis!   55

42.1. SD, 43.1. SD] *This ed.; There is a golden shower, from which the nymphs*
appear in human shape. / *Edge (following line 43 this ed.); Enter* NISA,
CELIA, *and* NIOBE. / *Daniel (positioning as Edge).* 46.1. SD] *This ed.*
52. Cupid] *Q; Cupid? Edge.*

39–40. *send down . . . worship*] The means by which the nymphs are
restored to their former shapes reverses the process by which they were
transformed. In 4.1 the foresters are told that 'there shall arise a thick mist'
(117), sent by the goddess of the underworld, suggesting the obscuring of
the nymphs' persons by infernal forces, whereas in this scene Cupid calls
upon Venus to send 'down' that 'shower wherewith [she was] wont to wash'
her worshippers, suggesting the cleansing of the nymphs by a celestial power.
The shower as the agent of transformation may derive from 'Cloacina', an
ancient surname of Venus, signifying 'to wash' or 'purify'.
    42.1. *A shower . . . above*] The text affords no indication of the mecha-
nism by which the spectacle was effected or the nature of the shower itself.
Bond suggests 'the drawing of a semi-transparent curtain, or perhaps a thick
shower of torn paper' (iii, p. 569), whereas Edge assumes that the shower
was 'golden' (see collation note), linking the transformation of the nymphs
to Jove's appearance to Danaë as a shower of gold. There is no indication
in the text, however, that the shower was golden, and the notions of deception and adultery associated with the story of Danaë are clearly inappropriate
here.
    47. *as amazed*] as if bewildered.

Montanus. Happy Montanus!

Silvestris. Happy Silvestris!

Ceres. Why speak you not, nymphs? This must be done, and
you must yield.

Nisa. Not I!   60

Niobe. Nor I!

Celia Nor I!

Ceres. Not yield? Then shall Cupid in his fury turn you again
to senseless and shameful shapes.

Cupid. Will you not yield? How say you, Ramis? Do your   65
loves continue? Are your thoughts constant? And yours,
Montanus? And yours, Silvestris?

Ramis. Mine most unspotted.

Montanus. And mine.

Silvestris. And mine, Cupid, which nothing can alter.   70

Cupid. And will you not yield, virgins?

Nisa. Not I, Cupid; neither do I thank thee that I am restored
to life, nor fear again to be changed to stone. For rather
had I been worn with the continual beating of waves than
dulled with the importunities of men, whose open flat-   75
teries make way to their secret lusts, retaining as little
truth in their hearts as modesty in their words. How
happy was Nisa, which felt nothing; pined, yet not felt
the consumption! Unfortunate wench, that now have ears
to hear their cunning lies and eyes to behold their dis-   80
sembling looks! Turn me, Cupid, again; for love I will
not!

Ramis. Miserable Ramis! Unhappy to love; to change the
lady, accursed; and now lose her, desperate!

---

78. pined, yet] *Fairholt;* pined yet, *Q.*   83, 99, 109.] *Edge supplies unnecessary SD / aside /, following SP.*

60–2.] The unexpected defiance of the nymphs echoes the refusal of
Semele in *Endymion* to bow to the dictates of Cynthia and accept Eumenides
as her husband (5.4.220–3).

64. *senseless*] unfeeling.

75. *importunities*] solicitations.

78–9. *pined . . . consumption*] was worn away, but was unconscious of
being eroded.

81, 98, 108. *Turn me*] Transform me.

84. *desperate*] without hope.

Celia. Nor I, Cupid. Well could I content myself to bud in   85
    the summer, and to die in the winter, for more good
    cometh of the rose than can by love. When it is fresh, it
    hath a sweet savour; love, a sour taste. The rose, when it
    is old, loseth not his virtue; love, when it is stale, waxeth
    loathsome. The rose, distilled with fire, yieldeth sweet   90
    water; love, in extremeties, kindles jealousies. In the rose,
    however it be, there is sweetness; in love, nothing but
    bitterness. If men look pale, and swear, and sigh, then
    forsooth women must yield, because men say they love;
    as though our hearts were tied to their tongues and we   95
    must choose them by appointment, ourselves feeling no
    affection, and so have our thoughts bound prentices to
    their words. Turn me again. Yield I will not!
Montanus. Which way shalt thou turn thyself, since nothing
    will turn her heart? Die, Montanus, with shame and grief,   100
    and both infinite!
Niobe. Nor I, Cupid! Let me hang always in the air, which I
    found more constant than men's words. Happy Niobe,
    that touched not the ground where they go, but, always
    holding thy beak in the air, didst never turn back to   105
    behold the earth. In the heavens I saw an orderly course;
    in the earth, nothing but disorderly love and peevishness.
    Turn me again, Cupid, for yield I will not!

---

85. could] *Q;* would *Fairholt, Bond.*

  88. *savour*] perfume.
  89. *his virtue*] its beneficial properties.
  95. *our hearts . . . tongues*] our feelings were obliged to conform to their protestations.
  96. *appointment*] command.
  97–8. *have our . . . words*] be obliged to think whatever they say. The image is drawn from the legal arrangement that bound an apprentice to serve a master for a set period of years. The passage is the last of the extracts noted by Pudsey, who substitutes 'my' for 'our' and 'yor' for 'their' (86v).
  99–100. *turn thyself . . . turn her heart*] direct your course . . . move her affections.
  104–6. *that touched . . . earth*] See 4.1.94–6n.
  104. *go*] walk.
  107. *peevishness*] malignity.

Silvestris. I would myself were stone, flower, or fowl, seeing
  that Niobe hath a heart harder than stone, a face fairer   110
  than the rose, and a mind lighter than feathers!
Cupid. What have we here? Hath punishment made you perverse? – Ceres, I vow here, by my sweet mother Venus,
  that if they yield not I will turn them again: not to flowers,
  or stones, or birds, but to monsters, no less filthy to be   115
  seen than to be named hateful. They shall creep that now
  stand, and be to all men odious, and be to themselves
  (for the mind they shall retain) loathsome.
Ceres. My sweet nymphs, for the honour of your sex, for the
  love of Ceres, for regard of your own country, yield to   120
  love; yield, my sweet nymphs, to sweet love!
Nisa. Shall I yield to him that practised my destruction, and,
  when his love was hottest, caused me to be changed to a
  rock?
Ramis. Nisa, the extremity of love is madness, and to be mad   125
  is to be senseless. Upon that rock did I resolve to end my
  life. Fair Nisa, forgive him thy change, that for himself
  provided a harder chance.
Celia. Shall I yield to him that made so small account of my
  beauty that he studied how he might never behold it   130
  again?
Montanus. Fair lady, in the rose did I always behold thy
  colour, and resolved by continual gazing to perish; which
  I could not do when thou wast in thine own shape, thou
  wast so coy, and swift in flying from me.   135
Niobe. Shall I yield to him that caused me have wings, that I
  might fly farther from him?
Silvestris. Sweet Niobe, the farther you did seem to be from
  me, the nearer I was to my death; which to make it more

---

110. Niobe] *Bond;* Nisa / *Q.*

109. *fowl*] bird.
110. *Niobe*] Bond's emendation of *Q* 'Nisa' is adopted here, since it is
Niobe's rejection of him to which Silvestris responds.
120. *for regard of*] out of respect for.
122. *practised*] plotted.
128. *harder chance*] worse fate.
130. *studied*] contrived (Edge).
135. *coy*] aloof.

speedy, wished thee wings to fly into the air, and myself   140
    lead on my heels to sink into the sea.

Ceres. Well, my good nymphs, yield. Let Ceres entreat you;
    yield.

Nisa. I am content, so as Ramis, when he finds me cold in
    love or hard in belief, he attribute it to his own folly, in   145
    that I retain some nature of the rock he changed me
    into.

Ramis. O my sweet Nisa, be what thou wilt, and let all thy
    imperfections be excused by me, so thou but say thou
    lovest me.   150

Nisa. I do.

Ramis. Happy Ramis!

Celia. I consent, so as Montanus, when in the midst of his
    sweet delight shall find some bitter overthwarts, impute
    it to his folly, in that he suffered me to be a rose, that   155
    hath prickles with her pleasantness, as he is like to have
    with my love shrewdness.

Montanus. Let me bleed every minute with the prickles of the
    rose, so I may enjoy but one hour the savour. Love, fair
    Celia, and at thy pleasure comfort and confound.   160

Celia. I do.

Montanus. Fortunate Montanus!

Niobe. I yielded first in mind, though it be my course last to
    speak. But if Silvestris find me not ever at home, let him
    curse himself that gave me wings to fly abroad, whose   165

---

154. sweet delight shall] *Fairholt;* sweete delight, shall *Q;* sweete delight,
<he> shall *Bond.*

    144, 153. *so as*] provided that.

    145. *hard in belief*] resistant to persuasion.

    149, 159. *so*] provided that.

    154. *overthwarts*] rebuffs, crossing of his wishes.

    156–7. *as he is like . . . shrewdness*] just as he is likely to experience some
shrewishness with my love.

    160. *confound*] destroy, dash.

    163. *course*] habit, customary procedure. The word may simply carry the
sense of 'turn', however, here.

    165. *abroad*] away from home.

feathers, if his jealousy shall break, my policy shall imp.
Non custodiri, ni velit ulla potest.

Silvestris. My sweet Niobe, fly whither thou wilt all day; so I
    may find thee in my nest at night, I will love thee and
    believe thee. *Sit modo 'non feci' dicere lingua memor.*   170

Cupid. I am glad you are all agreed. Enjoy your loves, and
    everyone his delight. Thou, Erisichthon, art restored of
    Ceres, all the lovers pleased by Cupid; she joyful, I hon-
    oured. Now, ladies, I will make such unspotted loves
    among you that there shall be no suspicion nor jar, no   175
    unkindness nor jealousy. But let all ladies hereafter take
    heed that they resist not love, which worketh wonders.

Ceres. I will charm my nymphs as they shall neither be so
    stately as not to stoop to love nor so light as presently to
    yield.   180

---

166. imp] *Bond;* nip *Q.* 170. believe] *Bond* (beleue*); beloue *Q.*
170. *modo 'non feci' dicere*] *Punctuation as Daniel; modo non feci, dicere / Q;
modo, non feci, dicere / Bond; modo, "non feci!" dicere / Edge.* 176. take] *Q; not
in Fairholt.*

---

166. *imp*] Bond's reading is adopted here in preference to *Q* 'nip' (see
collation note) as it sustains the imagery of the passage as a whole ('imp' =
to mend the wing of a bird by the engrafting of feathers). Niobe asserts that
if Silvestris plans to curtail her excursions by restricting her movements, she
will circumvent him by some contrivance. Manuscript 'nip' and 'imp' are
easily confused.

167. *Non custodiri . . . potest*] No watch can be set o'er a woman's will
(Ovid, *Am.*, iii, 4, 6). The Loeb text reads: *nec custodiri, ne velit, ulla potest.*

170. *believe*] Bond's emendation (beleue = believe) is adopted here in
preference to *Q* 'beloue' (see collation note) as it avoids an empty repetition
and conveys Silvestris' willingness to turn a blind eye to Niobe's flights from
home.

Sit modo . . . memor] All that you need is a tongue that remembers 'I did
not do it' (Ovid, *Am.*, iii, 14, 48); i.e. Silvestris is ready to accept any pro-
testation of innocence.

172. *of*] by.

175. *jar*] dispute, quarrel.

178. *charm*] conjure, solemnly charge.

178-9. *as they . . . stately*] that they shall neither be so haughty.

179. *light*] frivolous, wanton.

presently] instantly.

Cupid. Here is none but is happy. But do not as Hippomenes
    did when by Venus' aid he won Atalanta, defile her
    temple with unchaste desires and forget to sacrifice vows.
    I will soar up into heaven to settle the loves of the gods,
    that in earth have disposed the affections of men.   185
Ceres. I to my harvest, whose corn is now come out of the
    blade into the ear. And let all this amorous troop to the
    temple of Venus, there to consummate what Cupid hath
    commanded.
Erisichthon. I, in the honour of Cupid and Ceres, will solem-   190
    nize this feast within my house, and learn, if it be not too

---

181. Hippomenes] *Daniel; Hippomanes / Q.* 182. Atalanta] *Fairholt;
Atlanta / Q.* 183. forget] *Fairholt;* forgot *Q.* 187. troop] *This ed.;* troupe
Q.

181–3. *But do not . . . vows*] Having won the fleet-footed Atalanta by out-
running her with the help of Venus, Hippomenes, a grandson of Neptune,
neglected to give thanks for his success, and was moved by the offended
deity to embrace his bride in a place dedicated to the worship of Cybele,
who, angered by his impiety, turned both him and Atalanta into lions. The
story is related by Venus to Adonis in Ovid, *Met.,* x. 648ff. / LCL 560ff. Lyly
regularly uses the spellings 'Atlanta' and 'Hippomanes / Hyppomanes' (see
collation note) when referring to the tale (see, for example, *England,* ed.,
Bond, ii, p. 88, line 13, and p. 130, lines 30–1.

183. *forget*] Fairholt's emendation (see collation note), adopted here,
depends upon the assumption that the lovers are the subject of a series
of injunctions. The verb may refer back, however, to Hippomenes and
Atalanta, who 'forgot' to sacrifice vows, but the lack of agreement between
'defile' and 'forgot' argues in favour of Fairholt's reading.

184–5. *I will . . . men*] Edge notes that this 'may signal an ascent' (p. 661),
and compares the passage to Venus' declaration to Cupid in *Galatea,* 5.3:
'you shall up to heaven with me' (line 107). In *Galatea,* however, the
comment does not herald either an immediate or spectacular exit, in that
Venus remains on stage throughout the remainder of the scene and leaves
the stage with the rest of the dramatis personae at the close. A comparison
between the two passages may, in fact, suggest that the lines in *Love's Metamorphosis* should not be taken as a stage direction, and that Cupid simply
retires into his temple at the conclusion of the scene. Compare Ceres' similar
delayed exit at line 201 following her announcement of intent at lines
186–7.

185. *that*] I who.

187. *blade*] flat leaf, prior to the development of the seed-head (ear).

to] proceed to.

late, again to love. – But you foresters were unkind, that
in all my maladies would not visit me.

Montanus. Thou knowest, Erisichthon, that lovers visit none
but their mistresses.　　　　　　　　　　　　　　　　195

Erisichthon. Well, I will not take it unkindly, since all ends in
kindness.

Ceres. Let it be so. – These lovers mind nothing what we
say.

Ramis. Yes. We attend on Ceres.　　　　　　　　　　200

Ceres. Well, do.　　　　　　　　　　　　　　*Exeunt.*

FINIS

201.1. FINIS] *Q; not in Fairholt, Daniel.*

194–5.] Montanus' response to Erisichthon's reproach is not entirely
truthful, in that, although the lovers have been preoccupied with their
amatory affairs, they have not been unaware of his plight. It is Montanus
himself who resisted the suggestion that they should visit him, claiming to
be fearful of the effects of his hunger (4.1.143–4). The exchange is designed
to exhibit not Montanus' mendacity, however, but the change that has taken
place in Erisichthon's relationship with others through his ready acceptance
of an inadequate excuse.

198. *mind*] attend to.

200. *Yes*] Ramis insists that the lovers are indeed attending to what Ceres
says (cf. German 'doch').

Index

Page numbers refer to the Introduction and Characters in Order of Appearance; act-scene-line numbers refer to the Commentary; 'n.' after a page reference indicates the number of a note on that page. An asterisk (*) preceding an entry indicates that the commentary note in this edition adds materially to the information given in the *OED*. Individual words appearing in various inflected forms are usually grouped under one form; phrases are indexed in the form in which they occur in the text. When a gloss is repeated in the annotations, only the initial occurrence is indexed.

QM LIBRARY
(MILE END)